VIRTUOUS WOMAN

The Life of a Proverbs 31 Woman

Virtuous Woman

The Life of a Proverbs 31 Woman

STACY HEADLAM-HAMILTON

CONCLUSIO
HOUSE PUBLISHING

Printed in Canada
First Printing, 2015

ISBN 978-0-9938420-9-2

Published by:
Conclusio House Publishing
10-8550 Torbram Rd.
Suite 430
Brampton, ON
L6T 0H7
www.conclusiohouse.com

DEDICATION

I dedicate this book to my two beautiful daughters, Stayan and Daidrea. My prayer is that one day you will both discover the virtuous woman within you that God has designed. Although there is no perfect woman, I pray you will strive to be your best, love your best, and give your best as the Lord leads.

Shout out to my handsome boys, Shadame, Dreon, Taimandre, and Daimareon. May the good Lord above bless each of you with a woman of virtue, someone who will stand by you, pray with you, and love you unconditionally.

To the man who has stood by me through the good times and the bad. I thank God for you, Daimeon! It was through our many trials that I began to seek God and desire to have the characteristics of a woman of virtue. I love you!

TABLE OF CONTENTS

INTRODUCTION

❧

As women, we are faced with many day-to-day challenges. We are mothers, we are daughters, we are sisters, we are providers, we are comforters, we are decision-makers, we are homemakers, we are advocates, we just *are*. At times, it may feel like we are the be-all and end-all of everything, and the challenges we face can be overwhelming. God's initial plan was for us to be helpers, but at times it can feel like there is more to our role than just helping.

This book is based on Proverbs 31, which replays a detailed conversation between a mother and her son. As the chapter goes on it describes a woman of many different capabilities, and the first thought that comes to mind when reading this passage is "Wow! What a woman!" As the Bible continues to speak of this woman, she appears to be perfect as there are no flaws mentioned. On one hand, reading it may cause you to feel like you are lacking in many areas compared to this "perfect woman," and on the other hand, it may cause you to think, "This is not possible." However, the virtuous woman is not about perfection but about being well-rounded and holding yourself to a higher moral standard.

Being a woman is not easy; I have learned that the hard way. God does not expect perfection, and He understands that we cannot do it alone. He knows and understands the struggles we face, the pain we feel, and every tear we cry. He knows us for our tender hearts, He's aware of the fears we have, and He understands the challenges that we face in our everyday lives. I wrote this book with the great expectation that when you have finished reading it you will be empowered as a woman and accept that although it is not an easy job, you are capable because God has already equipped you to be a virtuous woman. I pray that as you read this book God will empower you to keep pressing on.

You are a woman of virtue.

CHAPTER 1

"A capable, intelligent, and virtuous woman—
who is he who can find her? She is far more
precious than jewels and her value is far above
rubies or pearls." (Proverbs 31:10, AMP)

We women are faced with many different challenges. Some of us are single, independent working women; some are single mothers; some are wives and homemakers; some of us play the role of mother and father; and some of us are wife, mother, and bread winner all wrapped up in one. No matter who you are or what lifestyle you live, one thing is very evident—our job is not an easy one. Although we would all agree with that statement, we were made with the capability to do all that we need to do.

The first word used to describe the virtuous woman in Proverbs 31:10 is "capable." The fact that this word is used as the first descriptive word is very important. Capable means to have the ability to accomplish. As women, we sometimes feel overwhelmed with the day-to-day tasks and responsibilities we have, but I encourage you to not be dismayed, you were made with the ability to achieve all that God has set out for you to accomplish. Being a woman of virtue is to strive to display the characteristics of a woman with high moral standards. It is to be a woman who can admit to her downfalls, yet hold her head up high, knowing she has overcome and is becoming better every day. The question asked in Proverbs 31:10 is, "Who is he who can find her?" which implies that this kind of woman is hard to come by. As we go from childhood to womanhood, the trials we face will become a part of who we are. How we decide to use those trials will either make us better women or bitter women.

Intelligence is the ability to have a good understanding or mental capacity, and being quick to comprehend. Developing intelligence comes from learning through some of the trials and life lessons you have faced in life. The key thing is to take from every trial and turn it into a learning curve that you can use to better yourself or use as a tool to motivate, encourage, and uplift another. No doubt, when you read about the virtuous woman in Proverbs 31, you get a feeling that this woman had probably been through some stuff. Having insight and reflecting on previous chapters in your life will result in a good understanding of what you want for your future and how you intend to get it. Every dream and desire begins with a vision. Your life will only seem hopeless if you have nothing to look forward to. Dreams become reality only when you begin to see the possibility of that dream. This all ties into having a good understanding and being quick to comprehend. Your past and present does not have to dictate your future.

Many women lose sight of a hopeful future because of past mistakes and becoming emotionally attached to a wrong decision that negatively affected them. We can't change the past, but we can certainly learn from it. We can't rewind time, but we can certainly plan for the time ahead. Reading Proverbs 31 and seeing the characteristics of this well-rounded woman, this woman of virtue, brings about the question, "How can we, as women, display these characteristics?" It is awesome to think that we could be considered more precious than jewels and more valuable than rubies and pearls. When we think of jewels, rubies, and pearls, we envision something beautiful and valuable. There are many different types of jewels; pearls come in many shapes, sizes, and colours; and rubies are precious stones that also come in many different shapes and sizes, they sparkle and shine and are attractive. What we see in these jewels, pearls, and rubies is the end result of a process. Let's take a few minutes to learn more about jewels, pearls, and rubies.

Pearls are formed when an irritant, such as sand or debris, enters an oyster. The oyster then secretes something called nacre to coat the irritant; this is what creates the pearl. The pearl must be left alone for several years to grow before it can be harvested. One of the most popular precious metals is gold. Gold must first go through a process of extraction. This is when the big pieces of gold are made into smaller pieces, and then a solution combined with air dissolves the gold to get rid of any other rocks or metals that are not gold. Refining is one of the last stages of the process. Refining is when the gold and a chemical called flux are heated to 1600 degrees Celsius. Rubies are made of a mineral called Corundum. The word ruby is derived from the Latin word that means red. All natural rubies have imperfections, and in order to improve the ruby's quality, heat must be applied. The heating treatment can be done at up to 1400 degrees Celsius in order to eradicate impurities. When you see the finished product of these beautiful pearls, jewels, rubies, and precious metals, you would have no idea of the process they had to go through in order to become what they are. What you see is the finished product. You see quality, value, and beauty, never having an understanding that there were imperfections, impurities, and a process of refining.

When Proverbs 31 speaks of the virtuous woman, it describes a woman who has been through a process to develop into a woman of quality and value, a woman who has overcome several years of growth and development, a woman who has been refined after going through some fiery trials—the application of heat in her life to eradicate impurities and help to improve the person she is becoming. Being a woman of virtue is not just about being a woman of high moral values, it is also about the things you have learned through your trials that contribute to making you a better woman.

Life is a journey that leads us through many paths. As we go through each stage of development, people and things will come along and make deposits into our lives. All of these contribute to our characteristics and the person we become. Although it may not seem like it at the time, it's the trials you endure through life that will make you stronger. Strength is defined as having the capacity to withstand great force or pressure. Yes, it may be painful; yes, it may be hard; yes, you may feel like you can't go on, but you have to have the ability to withstand in order to see what lies on the other side of the chaos, disappointments, struggles, and pain. Whatever it is that you have been through, are going through, or will go through, is to make you stronger, build character, and mold you into what God wants you to be. James 1:2-4 says, "Consider it wholly joyful, whenever you are enveloped in or encounter trials of any sort or fall into various temptations. Be assured and understand that the trial and proving of your faith brings out endurance and steadfastness and patience. But let endurance and steadfastness and patience have full play and do a thorough work, so that you may be perfectly and fully developed, lacking nothing" (AMP). Many may read this passage and wonder how trials can be considered as joyful. James is not saying to be happy while you are going through trials. What he is saying is to look beyond the here-and-now and consider that the situation goes much deeper than the trials themselves. Every trial you go through is another stage of development and character building. Anything that will add value to your life is going to take some patience and steadfastness. There is a saying that the race is not for the swift but for the one who endures to the end. Making the decision to give up is ultimately the reason one will lose the battle. Many times, while going through trials, we wonder why and plead with God to take us out. We feel burdened and dismayed, yet God has already promised that He will take our burdens and make them light, but we need to hand them over to Him. We have all been through times when we are frustrated with God. He says that we are to hand it over to Him, yet it seems like the weight is still on our shoulders. God has every trial we face figured out. He knows the end of the chapter. He is not on His throne trying to figure out how He is going to get this under control; He already has it under control. He wants you to trust Him and know that He is still the author and finisher of your faith. Take from each trial and tribulation, and figure out the lesson you should pull from it to help build your character as a virtuous woman. God has a purpose and a plan for you. He wants to build you up and draw you into a closer relationship with Him. It is often in our brokenness that we truly come to know God.

I absolutely love the story about the woman at the well, the Samaritan woman. This is one of the most touching stories about the compassion and love that

God has for each of us in spite of who we are or what we have done in life. His purpose is not to use your past to crucify you, but to use your downfalls to show how you can change in His hand. This story is told in John 4 after Jesus baptized some of His disciples. He had left to go to Galilee from Judea, but he needed to go through Samaria. He stopped at the well that Jacob had there, but Jesus never took any water to drink from the well. He just sat there. It wasn't until the Samaritan woman arrived that He then asked her for a drink. She replied with shock because the Jews never had anything to do with the Samaritans. She asked Him, "How is it that you being a Jew ask a drink from me, a Samaritan woman?" Jesus replied to her by saying, "If you knew the gift of God, and who it is who says to you 'Give Me a drink,' you would have asked Him, and He would have given you living water." She went on to have a conversation with Jesus about this water, this living water that will cause her to never thirst again after consuming. She then asked for this water and He said to her, "Go and get your husband." Confused about the switching of topics, she said, "I have no husband!" Jesus replied, "Yeah, I know, you have five of them." She then said to Him that she believed He was a prophet because He seemed to know a lot about her life, even though He was a stranger.

What is the lesson here? It wasn't a mere coincidence that Jesus went through Samaria, sat at the well, and was there when she arrived. Jesus set out on purpose to be there for her, and He offered Himself to Her. She lived a life that was not perfect. Yet, although He acknowledged all that He knew about her, He did not judge her or crucify her. He made it known to her that He had knowledge of her lifestyle, and then He offered her a way out. The fact that Jesus awaited her arrival is a clear illustration of His ability to wait for us. He is there to offer His hand of help, but we first need to acknowledge our need for a Saviour. The woman at the well could have rejected Him and walked away, she could have denied that her lifestyle was not pure, but she did not. She was willing to admit that there were impurities in her life, and she desired to know more about this water that Jesus had to offer.

Many times, when trials come into our lives, it is God's way of washing away some of our impurities. He wants us to acknowledge our need for Him and recognize that He is there at the well waiting for us to come and meet Him in our time of need. The woman at the well came to the well for water to quench her thirst, 'a fix it for now,' but when she got there, Jesus was waiting for her to give her something that would add value to her for a lifetime—the Solution. I am in no way implying that a relationship with the Lord is the answer to never having trials in your life again, but I am guaranteeing you that the trials you endure will be much easier to handle with Him in your corner. The reason I love the story of the Samaritan woman so much is that it shows God's ability to meet you where you are in your life's journey. He lets us know that He knows all about us, yet He is still willing to be there for us.

The meeting at the well also signifies God's ability to wash away our impurities if we allow Him to. Notice

Jesus never said to the Samaritan woman, "You have to drink the water I have." He offered it to her, and it wasn't until she showed interest that He then told her about the husbands she had. It was important to tell her about the husbands as His way of indicating that she must first acknowledge the impurities in her life before they can be cleansed away. Sometimes, trials come as a result of living a life outside of God's plan. And many times, in order to turn it around, He will allow it to fall apart since we think we have it all figured out. Once again, I am not implying that every trial you go through is because you have done something wrong, but many trials we go through have a lot to do with what we have done outside of the will of God.

God will allow some situations in your life to refine you. He will allow us to go through some messy stuff for us to be fine-tuned and better than how we started. He's not surprised about our past, nor is He concerned about our future. He knows the end, but it is up to us to make the decision as to whether we want what He has to offer or not.

Jesus saw value in the Samaritan woman. Despite her past and how she was living her life, He saw worth in her. He sat at the well awaiting her approach so He could assure her that she did not have to journey through life alone. He sat there to assure her that He would be there if she needed Him and that He was willing and waiting to help her. Jesus went to the well, but He had nothing to draw the water up with. Now, the Bible doesn't clarify if she had her own bucket for her water, but I assume if she had, she would have used hers to get the water. If it were the case that neither of them had buckets, then it would be a clear indication that whatever drew her there was more than her thirst for water to drink. Sometimes, God is in the midst of the trial you are going through because He wants to draw you to Himself. It is the process of refining, it is the heat application to turn you into what He has envisioned for you, into that woman of virtue that is far more precious than jewels and whose value is far above rubies and pearls.

Earlier in this chapter, I gave some details about the process that rubies, pearls, and jewels go through. Let's think for a moment, if these raw materials were taken in their natural state and placed in a shop for purchase or for assessment of value, just imagine what they would be worth. No one would invest in these raw materials unless they had knowledge of the worth of their end result. When God sees you, He sees the end result. He understood from your birth that, like the rubies, there would be impurities, like the gold, there would need to be refining, and like the pearls, you would take several years to grow. Nothing you have been through, are going through, or will go through comes to God as a surprise. The people who take these materials and invest time in the process do so because they understand their value even before the end result. It's not about what you see in the present, rather it's about seeing beyond the present and knowing that better is ahead.

I encourage you, woman of virtue, to keep pressing on. If you find that life has thrown you some trials and you feel overwhelmed or discouraged, don't you give in and don't you give up. You are going through a process of development, the stages of refining. Know that you are not alone, there is someone sitting at the well awaiting your arrival, one who knows all and has the ability to give you what you need as you journey through life.

A capable, intelligent, and virtuous woman—who is he who can find her? She is far more precious than jewels and her value is far above rubies or pearls. She's a woman of persistence, a woman that never gives up, a woman of beauty, a woman of respect and dignity, a woman who has made some mistakes but is determined to learn and grow from them. She is a woman hard at work to achieve, a woman of prestige, self-worth, and self-respect. She is a woman.

You, woman of virtue, press on and go forward, don't allow life's circumstances to dictate your path in life. Take control and take charge, be determined to see it through to the end. When and if you find yourself discouraged, as though you can't go on, find worth and value in who God has created you to be. Don't feed into a lie that says it will never get better. Find value in anything that is positive, even if it is small, grab hold of that piece of hope and watch God use it to flourish in your life.

The Bible says that faith as small as a mustard seed is all you need (Luke 17:6). A mustard seed is a very tiny seed that is used in various foods and spices. The point of having faith as small as a mustard seed is to signify how much of a difference a very small amount of faith can make. It is when one feels like there is absolutely no hope that life seems hopeless; and when life seems hopeless, that is usually when one feels like life is not worth living. Seeing that little ray of light (the hope for something better) at the end of the tunnel will allow you to have hope that what seems like a long journey will eventually come to an end. Have faith in knowing that better is coming, be confident that trouble will not always last, be assured that there is a God who sits on a throne and has control over everything you endure throughout your lifetime. Even when it seems like He has taken a backseat and is watching you suffer, He is in control and working it all out for your good.

Jeremiah was a man in the Bible who endured some persecution himself, but God told Him, "Before I formed you in your mother's womb I knew you; before you were born I sanctified you; I ordained you a prophet to the nations" (Jeremiah 1:5). The point was to reassure Jeremiah that there was already a plan set in place before his life began in the womb. God does not intend for your life to be chaos or for you to live in turmoil. He has already orchestrated your turnaround, and He's already finished the end of your story. It's for you to take the necessary steps to get to the finish line.

You may not be going through much of a trial in your life right now, it may just be that you are feeling unfulfilled or like there is more to life than what you're living. The truth is that we can all be better, live better, and do better; there is room for improvement in all of us. A woman of virtue is not one who has it all figured out, rather she is one who is still figuring it out. A virtuous woman is a woman who is consistently working to achieve the best moral standards in every situation. Part of that character building is to learn to display the very characteristics that Jesus has displayed through His love for us. Being a woman of virtue is not so much about the characteristics you display so that others may boast about how wonderful and well-rounded you are, but it's the ability to hold your head up high and walk with confidence, knowing you are someone who can be respected and admired for the sincerity of the characteristics you portray. It's about more than just the outer display of beauty and the visual picture one sees with the natural eyes. It's actually about the cleansing and purification and filtering of the inside that reflects who you truly are and your true beauty.

What am I saying? As women, we take time and pride in creating an illusion of how we want people to perceive us. We spend hours combing our hair, picking the right outfits, putting on makeup to disguise what we feel are flaws, we spray on perfume to smell our best, we spend a lot of time getting it all together, yet seldom do we invest the time required to build who we are on the inside. This is truly where our beauty begins. Have you ever seen a very physically beautiful woman who has a rotten attitude? You will often hear people say that her attitude makes her ugly. The point to all of this is that there is not enough emphasis on the importance of character building as there is on beautifying the outer being of a woman.

The Bible tells us that we are all made in God's image,

and at the end of the day, we are all beautifully and wonderfully made in His eyes. With age and time, our outer body will start to change, our looks will become old, and no amount of makeup or plastic surgery can ever rewind our aging process. It is all an illusion. The only real thing that matters is who we develop inside our physical bodies and how we live the life that God has given us.

Who can find a virtuous woman, one who is righteous, good, moral, ethical, irreproachable, blameless, honest, and incorruptible? Seems a bit extreme? Is there even such a woman? This type of woman lies within each of us. We are all capable of displaying these characteristics. Yes, we are! Although no one is perfect, apart from God, the virtuous woman is described as capable. Therefore, we have the ability to display all these characteristics if we work at it. No one is saying that you have the ability to be perfect, but you have the ability to change and become a well-rounded woman with help from God. Some may wonder what the big deal is and may feel that there is no significance, but I assure you that it is a big deal, and who you are as a woman has an effect on those around you. Why do you think that King Lemuel's mother thought it was necessary to have this talk with her son about a woman of worth? As she gave him some words of wisdom, she spoke to him about the value of the woman worthy of her son. Go figure that a mother would want a wife of pure perfection for her son. No one is usually good enough for a mother for her son. We know how that goes. The fact that it was the mother of a king who spoke about this woman of virtue also illustrates that these qualities are that of a queen. This is just another insight into how God sees us.

Working on the characteristics of a virtuous woman starts with self-evaluation. The woman of virtue was not born in perfection, but through the journey of life, life's lessons were used to build her character. Many may see you and have an opinion of who they feel you are as a person, whether that be good or bad. It is for you to search within yourself and evaluate who you are and who you want to be.

Life has a way of being unpredictable, and sometimes the hardships you face may seem unfair. Grab hold and have a clear understanding that you cannot control some things in life, but you can control how you allow those things to affect you. Sometimes, we can be our own worst enemy. Being a mammal full of emotions, we sometimes tend to react and behave based on our feelings, which sometimes, if not most of the time, is not the best thing. We women *do* because we feel, and we *don't do* because we feel. Understanding the effects of our emotions can help us to comprehend why some battles we face are hard to overcome. The reality is that if we desire change, we must understand what needs to change and what we need to do in order to change it.

Doing the same thing a different day will still produce the same results. Self-reflection is a very important starting point, regardless of what you are facing. Whether it is a trial you are going through or changes you want to make in your life, self-reflection acknowledges where you are and directs you to where you need to be. Therefore, take time out to reflect on yourself. Are you the person you desire to be? Are you truly happy with the person you are? Do you see any area of your life that you can improve on? Are there characteristics that you need to work on? Answer the question for yourself, "Who am I?" Are there things or people in your life that need to be filtered out? How do you measure up to the woman described in Proverbs 31? Being that there is none perfect besides God, I assume that there was at least one question that had you thinking from that list, and at least one thing that you could benefit from changing in your life. Now that you have reflected a little on yourself, the question is, do you find significance in changing that thing or those things?

The woman at the well acknowledged that she was living a life that had some imperfections. She was then made aware that those things were no secret to God, and although He knew the things He knew about her, He was there with loving and open arms, waiting for her.

God is able to meet you at any point in your life, He will never turn His back on you, nor will He reject you. God sees worth and value in you. The beauty He sees goes beyond skin deep. Just like those who value the rubies in spite of their imperfections, just like those who wait with patience for several years for the process of the pearls to come to completion, if it was not for value they would not waste their time. God sees value in you, and like the gold, He is refining you so that you will come out looking your best, shining with great value and worth.

Chapter 2

"The heart of her husband trusts in her confidently and relies on and believes in her securely, so that he has no lack of gain or need of spoil." (Proverbs 31:11, AMP)

If you are not married, you probably feel as though this chapter is not for you, but you are mistaken. This verse does not only address the married woman but also the woman who is hoping to be married someday. Developing the characteristics of the virtuous woman before marriage is as important as having them while married. When a man makes the decision to settle down with a woman, it is the value that he sees in her that makes him want to claim her for himself. There is a saying that "behind every good man is a good woman." We may not consider the importance of our role in partnership with our husbands, but God was aware of it from the very beginning. In Genesis 2:18, God decided that it was not good for the man to be alone, and He created woman by taking one rib from the man and placing it inside the woman. God could have very well created a woman without using one rib from the man, but there was a symbolic purpose in God's decision to create a woman from the man.

The ribs enclose and protect the heart and lungs, which are the vital organs. The frame of the ribcage supports the muscles of the chest, shoulders, upper abdomen, and back. Its flexibility aids the breathing process. Knowing the important function of the ribcage, it is no surprise that God used one rib to create a woman from a man. Metaphorically, the importance of the rib reflects the importance of a woman to a man. God could have used any other organ to create a woman, but the fact that He chose an organ that acts to protect, support, and help with breathing is very symbolic. The woman was made as a vital part to a man's life. As women, our function is highly important, and just as all organs need to work together to achieve the overall function of the body, women are important to the overall function of their husbands' lives.

God created us to be helpers, not in a sense that we may be demeaned or disrespected, but we are to stand in partnership with our spouse. When God placed Adam in a deep sleep to create Eve, He created them in equality. God took the rib from the man and created a woman to symbolize the intention of unity right from the very beginning. God then said that a man should leave his mother and father and be joined to his wife, and the two shall become one flesh (Genesis 2:24). God not only used a very clear example of the intention of unity through His creation of man and woman, but He also allowed women to carry men in their bodies through the process of conception. Very intricate and well planned, this was no coincidence.

The job of a virtuous woman is to discover and learn how to partner with her spouse in order to have a marriage that is favourable in the sight of God. We are quite often consumed with our daily lives and completing tasks for the day that we miss the importance of forming and maintaining one of the most crucial relationships we will ever have. We are called *woman* because we were taken out of man (Genesis 2:23). God's decision to make us was so that men would not be alone. Many men will say, after being married for years and having children, that they feel alone and neglected by their wives. While it is important not to neglect our duties, we must consider how much some of the tasks we take on may affect our relationship with our spouse. Have we completely neglected our duty as a helper, for which we were made? If you meet a man who has a wife that is in sync with him—a woman who respects and honours him, one who listens and values his opinion, a woman who is wise and considers her thoughts and words carefully, one who is not afraid to give an honest opinion, yet is humble, one who says "We will try again," as opposed to "I told you so," one who refrains from pointless arguments, one who says "I love you" just because, one who puts him first—you will find a husband who confidently trusts his wife.

As I read and reread proverbs 31:11—"So he will have no lack of gain"—I wondered what exactly King Lemuel's mother was referring to. The virtuous woman was not just well-rounded in her own personality and character traits, but she was also a well-rounded wife. She was one who considered her wifely duties as important. The fact that he will not lack says it all. As a woman of virtue, the role of a wife is to be taken seriously. When we get married, we do not go home with a booklet on how to be the 'perfect wife.' With that said, we still have the ability to seek insight on how to be the best wife that we can be. Many times, a marriage fails because neither party cares to find out their role within the marriage. While the Bible is clear on the man's position within a home, it is also clear about the role of the wife. Being a woman of virtue is to strive to be the kind of wife a husband can trust, rely on, and be confident in, one who will support him, pray with him, love him, and be there through it all. This may mean to lend an ear when he has a rough day at work, instead of bombarding him with the difficult day you had as soon as he walks through the door. It may mean having a hot meal sitting in the microwave when he gets in, instead of him coming home from a long day's work and asking "What's for dinner tonight?" and you replying, "I don't know, look what's in the fridge!" It may mean that instead of feuding about something you both can't agree on, you suggest praying. It may mean that, even though you feel like he is wrong about some things, instead of trying to make him see everything your way, trust God to reveal to him what he needs to see. Let him see love, feel love, and know he is loved unconditionally.

She comforts, encourages, and does him only good as long as there is life within her (Proverbs 31:12, AMP). A woman of virtue carefully considers the feelings of her loved one. Your husband should be a reflection of the type of woman standing by him, one who is confident, content, and fulfilled in his relationship with you. Although you may despise it when a man compares you to his mother, this is the only other woman he will have in his life that will love him to the extent that he feels he needs to be loved. The comparison is not often meant as an insult, it is most often intended as a way to express something he feels he lacks. As much as many men display a macho exterior, they love to feel comforted; they want to be encouraged, feel appreciated, and be recognized for their hard work. A woman of virtue should be appreciated, but must also learn how to appreciate.

Woman of virtue, pray for your husband. Let him know that you are there to support him. He must feel that even if he falls, you will have your hand extended to help him get up again. One of the most effective ways to help your husband is to be a wife that prays for her husband. Take time to compliment your husband, show him affection, and be his number-one cheerleader. Don't just tell him he is appreciated, find ways to show him.

The virtuous woman is one who does her husband only good, as long as there is life within her. This statement is a clear indication that you should be in it for the long haul. Loving, comforting, and encouraging your husband is just the beginning, the woman of virtue is committed to her husband until death. Learn how to love your husband unconditionally. Know and understand what it means to display the kind of love that is not conditioned by his behaviours or actions. If you are married, building a strong marriage is vital to your role as a woman of virtue. If you are not married, these characteristics are great to have, so that when Mr. Right comes along you are well prepared for a great partnership.

There is nothing like the comfort of a woman to a man. When a man feels like his wife is there to comfort and encourage him, it makes him feel valued. God has placed you to be your partner's cheerleader and his right hand. We are here to encourage and comfort our spouses through the best of times and the worst of times. The instructions were for a man to leave his mother and father and cleave to his wife and for the two to become one flesh. Becoming one flesh with your husband is to be so connected that nothing can separate or tear you apart. The family begins with the strong relationship you develop with your husband and the ability to make God the centre of that relationship. Many marriages fail because of the lack of communication between the couple, selfishness, and neglecting to bring the issues of struggle before the Creator of this union called marriage. Although it takes two to participate in making and maintaining a strong marriage, as a virtuous woman there are many things you can do without the participation of your spouse. What are God's expectations of you as a wife? Exactly what does it mean to comfort and encourage your husband? Consider your ways and carefully review the things you need to work on to be the wife that God has called you to be.

In everything and in all situations always remember to pray. Praying gives you that great communication with God that no one else can give you. Prayer helps when you need clarity, when you need strength, and when you need guidance. Developing the characteristics of the virtuous woman who comforts and encourages and does good to and for your husband, as long as there is life in you, means you are committed. You're committed to seeking God's will for you as your husband's wife. You're committed to loving, even if you don't feel loved. You're committed to praying, even when you're not sure why you should. You're committed to standing behind your husband, even when you feel uncertain about some of the decisions he makes. Make your husband a priority after God. Value him, appreciate him, and let him see that you respect him.

Many things in life bring feelings of uncertainty, but the husband of a virtuous woman should be certain that he has a woman who will be there to comfort and encourage him, no matter what obstacles life throws their way. Your husband should feel so comfortable with you that he feels no need to turn to someone else for comfort or encouragement. The woman of virtue may recognize that her husband has flaws and his ways may not be perfect, but she is committed to loving and encouraging him anyway. Many times, as women, we love to express how we feel about a particular situation and we, although seeing that it never works, continue to nag our husbands, feeling if we do it enough he just might change his ways or mind about that particular thing. We fail to realize that men usually do not respond to this behaviour. In fact, many will react opposite to how we want them to, just to prove their view is correct. Sometimes, even if you feel you are right, instead of trying to push your opinions on your husband, pray for him, encourage him, and allow God to direct him in the right path. Remember, the first relationship that man had was with God. You were not placed here to become your husband's director; you were made to help. Ultimately, God is the creator of man. If your husband is making some decisions that concern you, hand it over to the One who created him. Let your focus remain on developing the character of the woman of virtue, one who can look into her husband's eyes and say, "I love you just because," "I am here for you always," "I am praying for you," "Together we can!" Be the kind of wife that he just can't get enough of, one whom he feels comfortable enough to cry with if he needs to, one with whom he can express his deepest feelings, one he is not ashamed to admit his failures to. Be the wife that he can say with all confidence, "Here is a woman I can depend on to be by my side and to love me unconditionally."

I want to take Proverbs 31:11-12 one step further. The Amplified version reads, "The heart of her husband trusts in her confidently and relies on and believes in her securely, so he has no lack of honest gain or need of dishonest spoil. She comforts, encourages and does him only good as long as there is life within her." There is another aspect of comfort for your husband. As important as it is to give your husband emotional comfort, he must not feel lack as it relates to his physical needs. I think most of us would agree that at times keeping up with our husband's hunger for physical satisfaction is just not feasible. We are consumed with our daily responsibilities, and sometimes the days can't end soon enough so we can rest. Now I know I hear a lot of "AMENS!" Women sometimes feel like this aspect of a marriage can become a chore, and we need time to fit this in. I have actually heard several married women say, "I've told my husband that we need to schedule a time," meanwhile the men are like, "Schedule a time to be intimate with my wife?" Yes, it can be overwhelming, especially since we may feel like we have worked all day and sometimes our husband has not helped one bit. And then our down time comes and we have to worry about him wanting to be intimate, which may feel like one more thing on the to-do list. Some of you may be thinking, "Please, God, when I get out of this shower, make him be sleeping!"

Intimacy with your husband should not feel like

a chore. He should feel no lack or need for anything, including intimacy with his wife. A man needs to feel connected with his wife, and one of the ways he feels comfort is when his sexual needs are fulfilled by his woman. Woman of virtue, consider the sexual part of your marriage as important; don't place it on the list of *have* to do, but make it a thing that you *want* to do. Sexual intimacy is one of the most important ways of connecting and expressing the emotional feelings you have. Stop treating it as a chore; rather look at it as an expression of love. Be creative and learn new ways to spice up your love life, and start to enjoy it. You may be surprised, maybe then he will be the one saying, "Lord, when I get out of this shower please let her be sleeping because I just can't keep up!"

God created intimacy to be enjoyable, not dreadful. Many women have lost their desire to want to have a fulfilled and enjoyable sexual relationship with their husbands because of the pressure they feel at the end of a long day. Change your view about the physical aspect of your marriage. Remember 1 Corinthians 7:5 says, "Do not deprive one another except with consent for a time that you may give yourselves to fasting and prayer; and come together again so that Satan does not tempt you because of your lack of self-control."

Satan has a way of setting sexual immorality traps. He's just waiting to catch the perfect moment of weakness. He's aware that one of the ways to defile a marriage is through the sin of adultery. Although I am a firm believer that marriages can overcome anything, we must be aware of the strong temptations that can arise from sexual frustration. If God was not aware that this problem exists, He would have never made a point to mention it. The union of marriage was always confirmed with consummation. This was the symbolism of the two becoming one in the most physical way possible. After being married for several years, many may agree that it is challenging to keep the fire burning the way it was the first time. With that said, never stop trying to find new ways to light the fire in your sex life with your husband.

I know that we women can feel unimportant and neglected by our husbands at times, and sometimes it may feel like our needs are not being met by them emotionally, which then makes it hard for us to want to be intimate. Let's face it, for most of us, if not all of us, sex starts with the emotional connection we feel with our spouse before the physical desire to be intimate. Instead of being frustrated about how clueless they may seem at times, we have the ability to use our creativity to create an environment that is desirable for both parties involved.

Think of creative ways to set aside some alone time for you and your husband. Maybe put the children down for an early bedtime and eat a candle-lit dinner with your husband so you can reconnect and spark conversations that have nothing to do with bills or anything that leads to stress. Have a bath set with scented oils and lit candles ready for him when he comes home from work, dress up in a little costume and give him a massage while you ask him how his day was, and let him offload while you listen. Take time, under a dimmed light, to express to your husband your desires that need to be fulfilled and what it means to you to be connected with him, not just physically but emotionally as well. You may be surprised to see what your efforts produce and how it may begin to make him sensitive to your needs and desires as you show him your commitment and efforts to fulfill his.

Making your husband feel like he is important and desired by his wife is something every man loves. This may seem like it's all about him, but the point is to take your eyes off yourself and place them on your spouse. The virtuous woman is about giving, not receiving, she is one who considers the feelings and needs of her husband before her own. The point in all of this is to develop a character of selflessness. Be a wife that is excited to learn new ways to pleasure her man, physically and emotionally.

The physical aspect of your marriage should be a healthy one. You may feel that your husband's sexual appetite is too much, in that case try to compromise and see how you can make things interesting. Take time out to listen to his desires and find out what he may feel is lacking in the physical aspect of your relationship. As he shares with you his desires, take time to think about them, even if they seem unreasonable. Think about them and respond to him with the intention to show him that you have heard what he has said and that your desire is to please him. Then, with a gentle and loving answer, express the things you feel you're not receiving from him and why that contributes to your struggle to fulfill his needs. Sometimes, woman of virtue, it's not so much *what* you're saying but *how* you're saying it to him.

Chicken is a protein that we regularly eat in my household. Although I change it up several times a week and do different dishes like pastas, if we have a dish with chicken and rice two days in a row my children will always say, "Oh, chicken *again*?" Even though there are many different ways to prepare chicken, they look at it as the same thing over and over again. Sometimes, we can view our love life as having the same dish over and over again. Funny enough, if we eat chicken two days in a row but I change the side we eat with it, I don't get the same response. It's the same meat, but with just a different twist to the meal. What am I saying? Find ways to spice up your love life. A little change in how you do things can make a big difference. Walk into a lingerie store, but don't pick up your typical nightgown, do something he would not expect. Now, I'm not implying to go way out of your comfort zone, but think outside of the box. Make him feel like you have made an effort to make and keep him satisfied. That may just mean that you are dressed up and looking your best when he comes home from work, and when he says, "Where are you going?" you say "Nowhere." There are so many little things that you can do to spark the flutters back into the heart of the man you made your husband.

I remember one Valentine's Day my husband had promised from the week before to take me out to dinner. On the day, I was excited because we hadn't been out alone in a while. I had purchased my outfit for our night out only to get a call in the afternoon telling me the night I was looking forward to was not going to happen anymore because he had to work late. As disappointed as I was, I thought to myself, "Why waste the day?" I knew he had to come home at some point, so I thought of a creative way in which we could still enjoy our Valentine's Day. I made a quick stop to the dollar store and purchased two candles, two fancy dinner plates, two wine glasses, napkins, and a container of red rose petals. I then stopped at the grocery store and picked up the items I needed to prepare a special Valentine's dinner for myself and my Valentine. When he came home, he was welcomed by a wife dressed to go out for dinner and his clothes laid out for him to wear after he showered. Once he was dressed, he came downstairs to a candle-lit dinner, the table dressed with a red bedsheet, sparkling wine, and a dinner unlike the usual dinners on a weekday. We couldn't go to the restaurant, so I brought the restaurant to us. I topped the night off by dressing the room with gorgeous red petals, and the rest was history.

At times, it may be a factor of not having the money to go out, but you don't require money to spend quality time with your husband. It may mean that on a weekend off on a hot summer day, you pack a basket of fruits and some sandwiches, go to the nearest park or even your backyard, and spend quality time with your husband. Try to make a big deal out of special occasions; it doesn't have to be expensive.

The wife who comforts, encourages, and does

only good to her husband is the one who will have a happy husband. A husband with a wife who loves him unconditionally, respects, honours, values his opinions, and puts him before herself, will say with confidence, "I trust her." A man who knows, without a doubt, that he can rely on and believe in his wife is one who will feel he lacks nothing at home. This is a man who has a woman of virtue by his side.

Consider your ways, woman of virtue. Don't be that woman who is hard to get along with, don't be that woman that causes a man to rather live on a rooftop than be in the comfort of his own home. Your husband should see that you respect him. A man values a woman who has respect for him. Your husband should never feel alone or deprived of your physical or emotional connection.

A man views his home as his domain, a safe haven, a place of peace and comfort. One way that you can help to make sure his experience of coming home is enjoyable is to make your house comfortable. Some men say that they are annoyed with a home that is unorganized and messy. Some say that their pet peeve is coming home from a long day of work to a house that is chaotic. How you keep your home as a wife says a lot to your husband. Sure there may be days when there is too much to do and not enough time, but make it a priority to present your home in a way that when he comes through the door he feels like a king entering into his castle. Comforting your husband also includes making sure he is comfortable in his environment.

CHAPTER 3

"She seeks out wool and flax and works with
willing hands [to develop it]. She is like the
merchant ships loaded with foodstuffs; she
brings her household's food from a far."
(Proverbs 31:13-14, AMP)

lax is a round, dry capsule containing several glossy brown seeds. Wool is the fibre that grows on the body of sheep. It replenishes itself each time the sheep is sheared, and it grows continuously throughout the lifetime of the sheep. Wool is used as a protective coat, and its fibres are resilient and not easily broken or damaged. Every fibre of wool has a natural elasticity and wave that allows for it to be stretched longer than three times its original length, then spring back to its original length. Its cellular structure allows it to absorb moisture but repel liquid. No other synthetic fibre is capable of having these combined characteristics. Wool is also the only fibre with a natural resistance to fire.

The analogy of the virtuous woman seeking out wool and flax and working with these items with willing hands goes deeper than what it appears to be. The woman of virtue is one who examines herself and evaluates her self-worth and self-improvements. She is able to acknowledge her flaws and imperfections as well as utilize her qualities of strength. The ability to strip oneself of pride and consider areas of improvement will ultimately result in the ability to change for the better. Sometimes it takes the honesty of self-evaluation to acknowledge where change needs to begin within oneself.

Notice that once the wool is sheared it replenishes itself and continuously grows throughout the sheep's lifetime. Stripping yourself of pride in order to self-evaluate does not mean that you should have feelings of condemnation or feel contemptible. The intent is to recognize the need to replenish and replace those former actions and characteristics, giving room for a better you. Not only does the wool replenish itself once it's sheared, but the growth is continuous. This fact is key. The growing process is not for a season, it's for a lifetime. Even at your best there is still room for growth and development. Beginning to change is only half the battle; it's the ability to continue to grow and change that is the real challenge.

It is true that life's circumstances and situations

play a part in how we react and develop some of our characteristics. Some people are able to face a challenge in life, and no matter how negative it is, they can utilize it and turn it around for a positive outcome, while others may drown in self-pity and be totally consumed and overwhelmed by the challenges they face. They are alive but not living because they have been bound and chained by the pressures of life. Wool is not easily broken or damaged; it is a coat of protection and its fibres are resilient. The woman of virtue is not one to give up. Her ability to spring back after a downfall is what makes her strong and determined. She won't be easily broken and will not allow her life's circumstances to determine her outcome. Woman of virtue, you have the ability to take control of who you are and how you live. Bounce back when you've made a mistake, re-evaluate, look where you've gone wrong and what you need to do to change the outcome of your situation going forward.

The fibre of the wool has a natural elasticity, allowing it to stretch and then return to its original form. It also allows moisture but repels liquid. Learn what you can from previous situations in your life. Absorb the lessons learned and use them for growth, but never allow them to destroy you as a person or dictate who you become. Repel those feelings of negativity that say you can't change and that you're not good enough. Repel those feelings of condemnation and don't hold on to the things of your past that you want to change but can't change. Repel the feelings of depression and worthlessness and every negative thing that will hold you back from becoming the woman God desires you to be. Yes, things happen, and sometimes it may feel like you are in a fire because you feel the burn, but just as the wool is the only fibre with a natural resistance to the flame, you too can walk away unburned. The fire may come, but it does not have to consume you. Woman of virtue, develop the qualities of wool.

The fact that the woman of virtue is seeking out wool and flax is important. There are many different components to flax, but everything begins with a seed. As mentioned earlier, the fruit of flax is a round, dry capsule containing several seeds. A seed is a small item that is planted and from which a new plant can grow. Seeds are the beginning elements for almost anything that requires a growing period to achieve an end product. Fruits, trees, plants, even the process of our creation began with the implantation of a seed. I can remember the very first seed I ever planted back in kindergarten. The class was excited when the teacher announced that we would be planting seeds to take home for our mommies for Mother's Day. We painted and decorated our small white Styrofoam cups, then we got the soil and filled the cup halfway, then we took our seed and had to poke the soil with our fingers to ensure it was deep enough in the soil. We gave it some water and then put it by the window for some sun. Every day we came to class and all of us little ones would run to the window, excited to see the growth of our new plant. But to our disappointment, after a day, inside our cups looked just the same as the day before.

We repeated the same thing day after day, gave it sun and a little water, but nothing happened. Can you imagine the impatience of little children coming to class every day to see some type of development of what we felt we laboured doing? By the time it was time to take the plants home, some of us were really disappointed that all we had to bring home to our mommy was a Styrofoam cup half-filled with dirt. It wasn't until several days later, after repeating the same process from school at home, that I could see a little tiny green bud. My plant was finally starting to blossom! At least that is what I believed. Eventually, when the plant became too big to stay in the cup, we removed it to put it in a pot and wow, there were so many roots. Who would have thought that, even though I saw nothing happening, there was much going on under the surface? Sometimes, woman of virtue, the seeds you plant will not always be visible to the naked eye, but as you deposit seeds and water and give them light, they will begin to grow roots, and before you know it, something wonderful will grow as a result of your efforts and patience to see it through. Woman of virtue, begin to plant your seeds of love, kindness, giving, peace, longsuffering, gentleness, forgiveness, self-control, and goodness. Water them with patience and give them the light of faith. In due time, you will see the product of a great combination.

A merchant ship is a ship that transports goods or produce. A ship is a water craft made to sustain the pressures of water and stay afloat. It's made to keep out water and anything harmful from coming on board.

Foodstuffs are any material used for or to prepare food; and food is any substance consumed to provide nutritional support for the body. Why would such a comparison be made? Why would a woman of virtue display these characteristics? The significance in having these characteristics is not so she may have all these great qualities to benefit herself, but it is because of what she can distribute and contribute to the well-being of others.

The woman of virtue considers the contribution she makes to the lives of others around her. She leads by good example, not claiming to be perfect, but demonstrating her desire to work on her imperfections. She is one who will set selfishness aside to embrace the needs of others, and while she may have needs to be fulfilled, she considers others before herself. She transports goods by the characteristics she displays— love, peace, joy and forgiveness. She encourages and considers words of wisdom before she speaks, she is able to pray for and with others, and she has the ability to reprimand wrong while displaying unconditional love and undeserving forgiveness. She wards off evil, not with revenge but through prayer. She protects those around her by carefully watching over things that threaten to harm them. She is one who withstands the pressures of life, not through self-pity and depression or a defeated attitude, but by being built like a ship with the ability to sustain and stay afloat.

Proverbs 31:14 says that the woman of virtue is like a merchant ship loaded with foodstuff and she is well prepared. She was not born with all these traits; rather she collected these attributes as she passed through hardship and pain, through hard work and perseverance, through falling and getting back up, over and over and over again, through being betrayed and having to forgive, through making mistakes and learning from them, through seeking and praying, through rejection and ridicule, through tears and loneliness. She is loaded with things from her past that have strengthened her to prepare her for the better things to come.

Woman of virtue, consider your past, not so you can rehash and hold on to bitterness and self-pity, but be like the merchant ship loaded with foodstuff so you can use all the materials of your life to prepare the food of strength, persistence, perseverance, wisdom, knowledge, faith, grace, mercy, forgiveness, love, kindness, forbearing, self-worth and self-value. This food is essential to your overall well-being. These attributes and how you use the past situations in your life will determine the outcome. Look at the process of preparing food, whether it is meat, rice, or pastries. These all require a process for an end result. Take meat for example, when you take meat out of a package, it has a raw smell to it, and if you were to place it on a plate straight from its package and eat it, there is a lot that could go wrong with your body. So instead, you spend time preparing it with seasonings, you may even marinate it in some kind of sauce to soak up the flavour. Yet still you require one more step prior to serving that meat—you need to place it under some heat, either on the stove or in the oven, and cook it for a particular time in order to consume this food in a safe manner. Have you ever tasted rice with no salt? How about undercooked rice or rice that had way too much water added to it? The point is that in order for food to be just right, it requires the right ingredients and preparation time. Food is needed to provide nutritional support, but if the food is unprepared or spoiled there is no nutritional value to it. The things that contribute to the nutritional aspect of your life are the things you can take out of the life lessons learned to build good character within yourself. You must discard the harmful stuff that is unbeneficial to you.

The foodstuff in the merchant ship is supposed to be transported, not left stationary. Likewise, use your life lessons to encourage others around you. Your life does not have to be perfect in order to help others in need of support. As you walk along life's journey, the point is not to think you can do it alone. Be willing to hold the hand of someone who is struggling or grab the hand of someone who is willing to support you. You don't need to do this alone in order to achieve.

Your food intake will determine the outcome of your health. While fried foods, baked goods, and sweet chocolates all taste and look great, consuming these things on a daily basis is dangerous to your health. Meanwhile, if you only eat lettuce every day, there is a lack of nutritional value there as well. Our bodies require a healthy balance to function at an optimal level. Woman of virtue, there *must* be balance. Strive to consume those things that provide spiritual, emotional, physical, and mental nutrition. Be well-balanced and prepared so you will have strength to withstand the challenges in life. And when a threat comes to try and sink your ship, you will be well-prepared for the storm.

Prior to sailing a merchant ship, the ship is inspected for safety. There is a process of evaluating the products that will be loaded onto the ship, the content of the products, as well as the weight. The importance of evaluating the things loaded onto the ship is to ensure they meet the legal requirements, and the ship's size must be able to withstand the weight of the products placed in it in order to avoid a shipwreck. The woman of virtue has a responsibility to self-evaluate. It is important to consider the types of things being transported to the people sailing along with her. Woman of virtue, consider your ways. Be careful of the advice that you give to others around you. Watch the way you influence the ones who may be looking up to you for advice or an example. Lead a life that can be honoured and respected, not because you're perfect, but because you have the ability to re-evaluate and adjust accordingly. Look carefully in your ship and inspect it for things that may be unsafe or harmful. Be one who can advise wisely. Live and lead a life with the ability to be objective and not subjective. Do not allow your feelings to dictate your actions and behaviours. Be one who can see the faults of others and address them with compassion instead of criticism. Be humble and mindful of the grace that God has given you, time and time again.

Woman of virtue, load your ship with foodstuffs,

the type of food that adds value and quality to your life and to the lives of those around you. Protect the people on board your ship by being mindful and aware of how you lead your life and what you instill in others. Woman of virtue, be determined to be the captain of your ship. Know the weight and value of the things you have on board and consider them carefully for quality and worth.

The direction in which the merchant ship is going is another important aspect to getting the goods and produce to the desired destination. No captain begins a journey without a destination in mind. Imagine receiving a call from a travel agent and that agent says to you, "Congratulations! You just won a trip. There is no cost to you, all you need to do is pack a suitcase and show up at the meeting point, and your destination will be announced upon arrival." You may be excited, so you arrive at the meeting point and there is a lineup to board the ship. You take a seat on the ship, and with great anticipation, you wait to hear your destination. The captain of the ship welcomes you and congratulates you for being one of the winners of this great destination trip. He begins by sharing his experiences and how he became a captain and obtained his license. You feel confident because you are now aware that this ship is being guided by someone with experience and a license to operate it. He then announces that he too has no idea where you're going. He says that he was never provided a map and does not know the desired destination. He tries to reassure you by advising you that things will be okay, he will just go along with the flow of the current, and he states he is confident that at some point you will get to the desired destination. At this point, I'm sure you would think that this man is out of his mind and that there is no way that you would continue to go forward with the idea of being on a ship with no destination in mind. Woman of virtue, to get to a destination there has to be a vision. Where are you going? Your experiences in life are a great way to build character. They give you the ability to advise others from what you have learned, but it has to go much further than that, it can't just stop there.

Woman of virtue, you must have a goal, something you are working towards achieving. It may not always be smooth sailing along the way, there may be rain and storm, the currents might be high, you may have to detour a few times because the original route has been blocked, but continue sailing along with your destination in mind. Where do you want to go? Your experiences in life help to build character. Your determination not to quit is what makes you stronger. Your ability to keep striving to become better adds value. Your ambition is what will make you a winner.

In order for a ship to withstand the storm, the materials it is made from must possess the capability to handle all the pressures of the sea. The materials must be waterproof, heavy enough to hold up weight, and solid enough to withstand a storm. When building a ship, many factors are considered. The maker of this ship needs to know the amount of weight intended to go on this ship, they also need to be aware of what the ship is intended for. What the ship is transporting will determine how the ship is built, what materials are used to build it, and the design and finished product. The building of your ship—your personality, your experiences, and your growth—is to help to prevent you and those around you from sinking and drowning. It is to be and to live out an example so that others may be encouraged by way of your testimony. Woman of virtue, consider the materials used to build your ship, are they strong enough to withstand the storms of life? Have you considered using materials to make your ship one that is waterproof and able to bear weight? Woman of virtue, consider your worth and what your destination will be, build your foundation with the truth of God's Word, waterproof it with a relationship with the Most High, be mindful of the weight it can hold, and do not hesitate to offload through prayer when it seems like it won't withstand the weight.

"She brings her household food from afar." What exactly does this mean? When I read this part of Proverbs 31:14, I began to think of the significance of a woman of virtue bringing food from afar. I then began to think a little deeper about food itself and the importance food plays in the functioning of our bodies. Although we eat on a daily basis, we rarely consider the actual food we consume and the purpose it plays in contributing to a healthy or unhealthy body.

Food is used by the body for energy, growth, regulation, and protection. The different types of food we consume, such as fruits, vegetables, meats, proteins, carbohydrates, and grains, all work towards the same common goal. The nutrients found in these foods work in our bodies to prevent and fight infection, build immunity, build and restore cells and tissues, develop muscles, help with our growth and development, help with the healing process, and produce the energy we need for everyday activities.

Why is the food that the woman of virtue brings from afar significant? What is this food that she brings? Consider the role of a virtuous woman. You are the food that feeds your family! What nutrition do you give the body (your husband, your children, your extended family and friends)? Just as food is vital to the body's overall health and well-being, the woman of virtue recognizes the importance of supplying the right types of food, spiritually, emotionally, and physically, for herself and her family. The food from afar is made up of those experiences from your past that have made you wiser. It is the way you conduct yourself as a woman of God and also your ability to support and pray for your loved ones. It is your continual growth in the Lord that inspires others to seek after the Lord. You may ask, "How is this food for your family?" The greatest influence you can have on someone is how you conduct and live out your own life. Therefore, your responsibility as a woman of virtue is to provide the nutritional elements to your household that will result in a well-rounded home. You should feed them with the fruit of wisdom and knowledge, the vegetables of well-rounded discipline and structure, the sweet taste of love and compassion, the bread of life from the Word of God, and the water of the Spirit of God through prayer and fasting.

Food preparation can be time-consuming and requires some effort and strength. I know we can also attest to times when fast food is our number one choice when we feel tired or pressed for time. However, if we consume these unhealthy choices on a regular basis, it is a fact that our bodies will suffer. Too many fatty foods and oil and sugar will result in diseases, such as high blood pressure, high cholesterol, diabetes, and a number of other serious diseases. As such, careful selection and preparation time are important when considering food intake. The ability to supply food from afar to feed your family comes through your preparation time and careful selection of the food you are preparing for consumption. Let me explain what I mean by this. A woman of virtue is one of great moral standards, not because she is perfect but because she can recognize her imperfections and is willing to continually work towards the standard of God's expectations of her. There is always room for improvement, but while you are improving, your job is to guide those who are where you used to be, and you do this by praying for them, encouraging them, uplifting them, loving them, and humbling yourself so God can use you in a mighty way.

The selection of food for your family will come from spending time in the Word and allowing God to reveal to you the characteristics of the Holy Spirit that will take you to the next level of preparation. You can only be prepared for something if you prepare. Many times in life we face things that come as a surprise to us and then it is difficult to deal with because we are caught off- guard. I am in no way implying that we can prepare for everything that happens in our lives; however, I am implying that we can be ready for anything that happens in life. Have I confused you? Look at the home you live in. A house is a structure that has wood and brick and all the things it needs in order to hold you and your family securely in it. While the house cannot stop the rain, blizzards, or snow storms, it can definitely withstand those conditions. Paul said in Philippians 4:11-12, "I have learned in whatever state I am, to be content; I know how to be abased, and I know how to abound. In all things I have learned both to be full and to be hungry, both to abound and to suffer need." Paul had encountered adversities and trials throughout his life, but He found His strength in Christ Jesus. In verse 13 he says, "I can do all things through Christ who strengthens me." Life can be overwhelming, and the responsibility as a woman of virtue is a huge one. The storms and trials in life will come, but our anchor, which is the foundation we find in Christ Jesus, is what holds us together. He is the one who gives you the ability to keep pressing on. Your preparation time with Christ Jesus is the ultimate ingredient in the food for your family.

While preparation takes time, most of the food we prepare has to be placed in or on the fire. Quite often as Christians we pray that God will help us build characteristics of the Holy Spirit, we pray for patience, we pray for the ability to forgive, we pray for all sorts of things, not recognizing that in order to have those characteristics there is a developmental phase. So how would we learn to forgive if we are never put in a situation to forgive? How would we learn to be patient if we are never put in a situation to wait? I am sure we are tested in many areas as wives, mothers, daughters, sisters, aunties, and friends. Most challenging, I am sure are those challenges we face right in our homes.

God has given us the responsibility to prepare the type of food that will nurture our families, not just in the physical but in the spiritual as well. There will be times when you feel your husband is not in alignment with God's will, you will be burdened with the mistakes your children seem to be making, and you will feel a heavy load of responsibility to keep it all together. I have heard many question God saying, "If men are to be the head, Lord, then why....?" No one said that a woman of virtue will have it all figured out, no one said it would be easy to follow in God's purpose for you, but know and understand that although it is not easy, you will see the fruit of your labour in the end. We have a responsibility to keep on praying and interceding on behalf of our husbands and on behalf of our children. God promises that not one of His words will return to Him void. When you are interceding you are doing so with great expectations that God will fulfil the promises in His word.

The cooking time (the hardships you face) is all a part of preparation for your family; and while you wait, your continued efforts, your continued prayers, your continued encouragement, your unconditional love, no matter how hard it seems, is critical. The stove may get really hot when cooking but you cannot turn it off, the heat is what will cook the food, and you cannot consume something until the cooking process is completed. Although some dishes take longer to cook than others, the true test of your efforts comes when it is consumed. While a meal may look and smell good, it is only when we taste it that we can get a true sense of the efforts put in the preparation of that meal.

Another important factor when consuming foods is the elimination process. As humans, if we do not eliminate, that very same food placed in our bodies can turn against us and attack our bodies as poison. What is my point in this? As woman of virtue, we need to intake spiritual food and then put these things to useful practice so that we and our families will benefit from them. Your children's lives can be changed by them seeing you work through problems and issues by prayer; they will see and learn and follow. Your husband's life may be changed when he sees your ability to handle a stressful situation by turning it over to the Lord and walking in faith. Your family will be led by way of your example, simply by seeing the elimination process—the product of your efforts, the way you live your life based on God's word. They will see what you have been consuming by what you have put out.

Just as food is vital to your body's survival, woman of virtue, you are vital to your home, and the type of nutrition you give should be for health and strength, protection, growth, and order.

CHAPTER 4

"She rises while it is yet night and gets (spiritual) food for her household and assigns her maids their tasks." (Proverbs 31:15, AMP)

Spiritual warfare is a must for every woman of virtue. There are many issues in life that we encounter on a daily basis, and we require guidance and direction. We need to pray for our husbands, our children, and those around us. This is the perfect opportunity to be alone in the presence of God and cry out with any concerns you may have, to take your burdens to Him and cast them at His feet with the assurance that the Lord has all the answers to every situation you face.

You may have wondered, as I did, why the night is the perfect time for the woman of virtue to get her spiritual food and assign her maids their tasks. I am not quite sure if the time of day is as important as the fact that she gets it done. But it may seem like the night is ideal. Any woman with a family will attest that the quietest time to get things accomplished, undisturbed, is when everyone has gone to bed for the night. You will be amazed at the difference it makes to wake up into a new day, prepared and ready for whatever the world throws at you.

The Bible speaks about putting on the armour of God in Ephesians 6:10-18 (AMP), which says:

In conclusion, be strong in the Lord [be empowered through your union with Him]; draw your strength from Him [that strength which His boundless might provides]. Put on God's whole armour [the armour of a heavy-armed soldier which God supplies], that you may be able successfully to stand up against [all] the strategies and the deceits of the devil. For we are not wrestling with flesh and blood [contending only with physical opponents], but against the despotisms, against the powers, against [the master spirits who are] the world rulers of this present darkness, against the spirit forces of wickedness in the heavenly (supernatural) sphere. Therefore put on God's complete armour, that you may be able to resist and stand your ground on the evil day [of danger], and, having done all [the crisis demands], to stand [firmly in your place]. Stand therefore [hold your ground], having tightened the belt of truth around your loins and having put on the breastplate of integrity and of moral rectitude and right standing with God, and having shod your feet in preparation [to face the enemy with the firm-footed stability, the promptness, and the readiness produced by the good news] of the Gospel of peace. Lift up over all the [covering] shield of saving faith, upon which you can quench all the flaming missiles of the wicked [one]. And take the helmet of salvation and the sword that the Spirit wields, which is the Word of God. Pray at all times (on every occasion, in every season) in the Spirit, with all [manner of] prayer and entreaty. To that end keep alert and watch with strong purpose and perseverance, interceding in behalf of all the saints (God's consecrated people).

As women of virtue, we must recognize that our strength and our ability to do things is not in being self-sufficient. Putting on the armour of God is fitting as nurturing wives and mothers since part of our desire is to protect. What better way to protect than by interceding through prayer? I want to go a little deeper and look at things from the perspective that evil spirits linger at night. When the woman of virtue decides to rise up while it is still night, she is preparing to battle with the forces of darkness. She has already recognized that her family may be subject to attack from the enemy merely because of their faith in God. Woman of virtue, you must arm yourself and be aware that there are forces of darkness that linger around, waiting for the perfect opportunity to attack. These attacks may be on your marriage, your children, your finances, your health, and ultimately your soul. Be alert and on guard. Although certain circumstances may appear external, let the truth be known that it is against principalities and forces of darkness that we wrestle. However, rest assured that you are not alone once you have armed yourself with the *full* armour of God. There is no partiality when it comes to a life that is led and directed by God. You will be a target once you have made up your mind to live as a woman of virtue. Although it may not be easy, you are not alone.

I want to speak to you for a little while about the importance of arming yourself with the full armour of God and what that looks like as you live as a Proverbs 31 woman. The full armour of God is described as girding your waist with truth. In other words, surround yourself with truth, the truth of God's word. Sometimes, you may be faced with decisions on how to handle a particular situation. It may be something that you struggle with regarding yourself, it may be regarding your spouse, or maybe it is your children. Initially, you may be struggling with that issue or circumstance and may be praying about it, but it may seem like there is no answer or resolution. So, what do you do? Surrounding yourself with God's truth would mean using the Word of God as a reference in that particular situation.

Let's look at an example. You're pressed about a situation regarding your husband. Maybe your relationship with your husband has not been the greatest and maybe you have been struggling with the feeling of not wanting to remain in a marriage with your spouse any longer. You've been praying for a long time and nothing seems to change, no matter how hard you pray, no matter how hard you try, and now you feel that there is nothing left to do but walk away. However, if you have girded your waist with the truth of God's Word, you would know that His truth is that a wife is not to separate from her husband (1 Corinthians 7:10) and that God hates divorce (Malachi 2:16).

Let's look at another hypothetical situation. Your child has been rebellious, and he has strayed away from the ways that you have taught him. He seems to be heading down the wrong pathway, and you have prayed and fasted for him. You have exhausted all possible alternatives and still it seems like the challenges are neverending. Girding your waist with truth would allow you to recognize that there is only so much you can do as a parent, and then the rest is up to our Creator. "Train up a child in the way he should go: and when he is old, he will not depart from it" (Proverbs 22:6). You do your best and let God do the rest! Continue loving and praying for that child while maintaining your teachings based on the truth of God's Word. Then have faith believing that God will do a great work in that child and bring them into right standing with Him.

I use these two examples to illustrate the point of using biblical references as a way to gird yourself with the truth of God's Word and reject the forces of darkness that are in opposition to what the Word of God says. This applies to any and every situation you face. The one question you should ask yourself is, "What does God's

Word say about my situation?" When you don't know the answer, seek and you shall find (Matthew 7:7).

Come on, woman of God, we need to be alert and aware of our surroundings, and we need to be prepared to stand in battle for our families. Gird yourself with truth, and put on the breastplate of righteousness. To be righteous is to be in right- standing with God. Use these opportunities to pray about anything you feel that God is trying to change in you, anything that requires confession and forgiveness. Always be willing to make things right with God before praying for others.

"Shod your feet with the preparation of the gospel of peace." Shod is a type of footwear, so in other words, you are to be ready to walk in the teachings of Christ Jesus. No matter what challenges you face, your footsteps should be ones that reflect the peace and righteousness of our Lord and Saviour Jesus Christ. As Christ walked the earth, His teachings always reflected truth, in love and peace.

"Above all, taking the shield of faith, with which you will be able to quench all the fiery darts of the wicked one." A shield is used for protection. Prayer without faith is useless. Faith is required in all we do. The Bible says that faith the size of a mustard seed is all we require (Matthew 17:20), but faith is required! Satan will always try to shake your faith by presenting things in the physical for you to see. There is a saying that "seeing is believing," but on the contrary, the Word of God says that "Faith is the substance of things hoped for, the evidence of things not seen" (Hebrews 11:1). It's through your faith that you pray for your husband, it's through your faith that you pray for your children, and by faith and with great expectation you believe that God can and will do even the things that seem impossible. "But without faith it is impossible to please Him for he who comes to God must believe that He is, and that He is a rewarder of those who diligently seek Him" (Hebrews 11:6, NKJV).

"Take the helmet of salvation and the sword of the spirit, which is the word of God." This is your best line of defence, woman of virtue. Your helmet of salvation is to protect you from the attacks that come from the enemy. A helmet is placed on the head to protect the head from injury, and the head is the protection of your mind (brain, thought process), and the mind is where Satan begins feeding you with his lies that are in opposition to the Word of God. You have the helmet of salvation and the sword of the spirit to ward off evil. You must feed your mind the truth of God's Word, which rebuts the lies of the enemy. It is important to take time to know the truth of God's Word, so that when the enemy comes in with lies we can refute them with truth.

"Praying always with all prayer and supplication in the spirit, being watchful to this end with all perseverance and supplication for all the saints." "Be prayerful in every situation; and in all circumstances, be watchful and have your spiritual eyes and ears sensitive to your surroundings. Don't be distracted and misled by what things look like, but be aware of Satan who is prowling around with an ulterior motive" (1 Peter 5:8, NIV).

Woman of God, submit your ways unto the Lord and allow Him to take full control. Humility and submission are a big part of being a woman of virtue. You were not called to be self-sufficient in this pursuit of living out a life of high moral standards. Your submission to God in all that you do first requires communication through prayer and then obedience with a humble spirit. You may be praying for or about some things, and in return God may require you to do things or behave a certain way that may be opposite to how you would normally behave or the way you would normally react. Some of these ways may require a lot of patience or swallowing of pride. It may be very challenging to go against that urge to handle situations by yourself instead of taking a back seat and waiting on God, but praying in the spirit means you have handed things over to God, and by faith you are saying, "God I trust you with all, in every situation, in every circumstance."

Woman of virtue, part of your assignment from God is to get on your knees and cover your household in the spiritual realm. You need to be prepared every day, for every day will bring new challenges. Have you ever realized that when you feel prepared for something it is not as stressful as when you are unprepared? Being unprepared brings about anxiety and frustration. I believe being prepared physically is just as important as being prepared spiritually. The woman of virtue not only got spiritual food for her household, but she also assigned her maids their tasks. Now, if you are like me, you may not have any maidservants to be assigning tasks to, and I am assuming if she was assigning the maids their tasks it would not be in the middle of the night. I believe that this is referring to her being prepared for the next day, organizing things to be done, so that when morning comes she is well prepared to take on the tasks of a new day,

I can attest that every time I organize things from the night before, I wake up in the morning feeling great about the day. However, I find that whenever I leave things until the morning, everything seems to frustrate me because I am unprepared. When it comes to women who have to multitask, it is easy to feel overwhelmed at times. If you are a woman who works outside of the home and who has a husband and children, or even if you are single, or a stay-at-home mom, preparing yourself ahead of time allows you to stay on top of things, and being organized will also give room for the unexpected things that may pop up in your day.

Being a wife, a mother, and a working woman myself, I understand too well what a challenge it is to complete daily tasks, from cooking, cleaning, homework, dirty diapers, wiping runny noses, to assigned tasks at work. Yes, there are days when I have wondered to myself, "What in the world have I gotten myself into?" I can remember feeling many times like there was not enough time, not enough days, not enough energy, and not enough patience to get everything done. It wasn't until one day, after being frustrated, that I began to think about how I was not utilizing the help available to me. I thought about why I wasn't assigning tasks to my other team players at home. Why did I feel the need to do it all on my own? I then realized that it was because I had a bit of fear that things were not going to be done right, and then I would have to do them again anyway. I was set in the way things were from when my children had to solely depend on me. I would do their laundry, clean up after them, spread their beds, make their lunches, do the dishes, and clean the house. Well, no wonder I felt overwhelmed. It wasn't until I started to realize that there was nothing wrong with assigning tasks to the other individuals in the home that the feeling of being overwhelmed lessened.

So, part of assigning maids their tasks is learning to delegate some things to the others within your household that are capable of completing age-appropriate duties. Part of organization is delegating specific tasks to specific individuals within your home. This may mean that before the children go to bed, have them pick their snack for school for the next day, have them sort out what they want to wear, down to their socks.

Find time to plan meals for the week, know what you want to eat every day for the next seven days. It truly does work. Every time I plan meals for the week, and I mean breakfast, lunch, dinner, and snacks, I also end up saving a lot more money because I only shop for the specific items I require for those meals. It also saves a lot of time. Not only does it save me from circling the grocery store trying to see what I need from a random list of items I have written down, but it saves me from the "Oh, let me buy this item because it's on sale" temptation. If it's not required for that week, I don't buy it.

Maybe you are reading this and thinking, "I don't have children so this does not apply to me." Well, that's fine, if you do not have children you may just need to learn to assign tasks to yourself. You may need to have a list of tasks to complete and number them from the most important to the least important, and give yourself specific times to complete each task. Many women complain about their husband's lack of effort when it comes to household duties, but before we talk about this, please remember that you were called to be your husband's helper. With that said, I am not implying that your husband is not to help around the house, but maybe your approach to having your husband help around the house needs to change. Most men would probably prefer to not do household duties, but I believe if they felt that their help was required, they would help.

In the earlier stages of my marriage, I thought I had the perfect husband shipped to me from Heaven. He worked, he cooked, and even helped out with the laundry. It was great! As the years went by and we had more children, I started to see that the responsibility of household duties started to weigh more on me, and I remember thinking, "Now is the time when I need the help the most!" When I made the decision to begin delegating tasks to others in our home, I would, in the most loving way, say to my husband, "Babe, can you do this while I do that?" And, most of the time, if not all of the time, it was done, and I believe my approach had a lot to do with it. I was going to him with an I-need-your-help attitude, instead of an I-do-everything-around-here attitude. Now, I know you know exactly what I'm talking about. There is nothing wrong with delegating tasks, but be sure to do it in the right way with the right attitude. Also, be mindful to appreciate the help as you work together with your family members as a team.

I believe another big part of task planning and preparation is finances. In order to have things organized, budgeting and spending is going to be a part of the overall picture. Financial planning may be something that is handled by your husband, and if that is the case that is wonderful, but make sure that you are willing and able to help him if needs be in this area. This may mean to keep track of payments that are coming up, bills that are due, and so on. You'd be surprised how fast the months zip by and how easy it is to miss or forget about bills that are due if you're not paying attention or planning accordingly. Assigning tasks can also mean to delegate your dollars appropriately. One of the most challenging things for a lot of couples is organizing their finances and staying on top of financial budgeting and spending. It took a lot of work in this area for my husband and I, and we are still working on that aspect of things. Knowing when to spend, how to spend, when to save, how to save, what the differences are between our *needs* and *wants*, when it is necessary to say no to that new car, new shoes, you name it. When thinking about delegating your dollars, you should be prepared ahead of time. Before the money gets into your account, allocate each dollar to a task. Some may find it easy to budget weekly, others may choose bi-weekly or monthly. When you choose to do it is not as important as choosing to do it.

Have a budget book or calendar. I like using a calendar. We post ours in a visible spot so we can glimpse at it every day, which reminds us of things coming up. Whatever your preference is, have things written down. Know when they are due, know whats coming in and what going out. Another important part of delegating dollars and being prepared is to set aside some money for emergency purposes. Now, I know that some may be thinking that they barely have enough to get by, and that may be true, but then assess if there is anything that you are currently doing that you can do without. Organizing an emergency fund will help with the unexpected things that will come up at some point; it's not a matter of *if*, it's a matter of *when*. Financial strain usually arises from that one time when something unexpected comes up and, believe me, it only takes one time to see that domino effect play itself out in your finances.

Woman of virtue, note that being prepared spiritually and being prepared for your daily activities is an important part of your role. Picture yourself as a soldier with God being the lieutenant, ordering your every footstep. Arm yourself with the full armour of God, and be ready and prepared for war against principalities and forces of darkness. Wake up each morning already prepared because you are organized and have assigned all tasks for that day. Just think of how good you will feel when you realize the difference it has made because you have taken the time to battle for your family through prayer, and you have prepared for them by organizing daily tasks ahead of time. I guarantee you, if you have made the effort to truly arm yourself with God's armour and your days have been organized with careful thought and planning, you will see big changes in the days ahead of you.

CHAPTER 5

"She considers a field before she buys or accepts it [expanding prudently and not courting neglect of her present duties by assuming other duties]; with her savings [of time and strength] she plants fruitful vines in her vineyard"
(Proverbs 31:16, AMP).

This verse may be challenging for many of us women. As we know all too well, we women can make impulsive decisions at times. I will be the first to admit that careful consideration before decision-making could have prevented a whole lot of mistakes in my past. At times, we can take on too many tasks at once without careful consideration of our priorities, and then we feel overwhelmed due to the heavy load of responsibilities we have. The woman of virtue considers her financial obligations and responsibilities, but most importantly, she is aware of the responsibilities and priorities she has within her home.

You must carefully consider your current obligations before acquiring other duties that may interfere or cause neglect to the things that are most important to you. Recognizing the importance of order within your home is important. God must be at the forefront of all you do. Your duty is to first commit all of your ways to the One who created you, and in doing so, you show God that you acknowledge Him as the priority in your life. Growing up, I was always taught to kneel down and pray, or bow my head and clasp my hands to say grace around the dinner table. Some may perceive that communication with God is supposed to be overly spiritual, with tongue-twisting words that are loud and powerful, designed to open the ears of God. But when the disciples asked Jesus to teach them how to pray, Jesus gave them a very simple prayer to say that addressed all things (Luke 11:1-4). God understands even the quietest, simplest, heartfelt words. It's not so much how you say it, but rather the effort you make to speak with the Lord in all sincerity about everything.

I start by speaking on prayer because I feel that this communication with God will allow for clear direction and guidance in various areas of the virtuous woman's life. I want to use a specific definition of field while addressing this part of the verse. A field is defined as a particular branch of study or sphere of activity or interest. You may have a professional field of study in law, healthcare, business, social work, teaching, or whatever it may be, but for this moment your field of professionalism as a Proverbs 31 woman is being and becoming a woman of virtue.

We were created to be available to help our husbands in their tasks so that as a team we succeed in living out a life full of purpose and fulfillment the way God intended us to. In this day and age we live in, women who are barefoot and pregnant are few and far between. Women are strong and independent, hardworking, self-sufficient, and many live lives without ever having to depend on a man to do anything at all. I am in no way indicating that liberation for independent women is wrong; however, I am affirming that the Word of God is true in the order of which we must live as wives and mothers in our homes. We must make these roles a priority over other obligations, including that of our profession. We must be committed to prioritizing our commitments with God, then our husbands and our children. And, if we have the ability to do more after completing what is required of us in these obligations, then and only then should the consideration of a new field be accepted.

It is easy to be distracted with priorities. Many times the obligations of working outside of our homes supersede the time spent completing our tasks and obligations at home. We tend to be so distracted by the pressures of paying our bills and meeting our financial needs and obligations that quite often our lives and decisions are dictated by our professional field rather than our field of being a woman of virtue. How many of you can admit to waking up in the morning already feeling exhausted from the night before, then scrambling to get the children off to school or daycare, while hoping you will not be late for work? You work a long day, committed to completing the tasks ordered by your boss, and at the end of the day you rush home to complete the tasks of preparing dinner, bathing children, helping with homework, and preparing for the next day. By the end of the night you are ready to ship the kids off to bed without much time for talk or play, and most likely frustrated because the kids are being kids. Still you have had no time for your husband because at this point his needs are not at the forefront of your mind because he can take care of himself. You are now ready to just hit the sheets, and I mean alone, muttering in your heart, "He better not come in this bed expecting anything, because I have a busy day at work tomorrow," or "He hasn't helped me with these children," or "I'm too tired." And the very same God that has given you life for one more day was nowhere on your priority or obligation list for the day. The family you love and care for was treated like an item on your to-do list. We do this while claiming that our hard work is for our family, but ask yourself these questions: What really matters to me? What things in your life are distracting me from my true role as wife and mother? Woman of virtue, we have to remember that it was the distraction of the serpent that first led Eve to eat from the tree that God had forbidden in the first place. If your obligations outside of your home take precedence over your duties as wife and mother inside your home, then consider the field before accepting it. And if you have already accepted it, re-evaluate and govern yourself accordingly.

A vineyard is a plantation of grape-bearing vines, and a vine is any plant that has a long stem that creeps on the ground or climbs by winding its tendrils around a support. The Amplified Bible says, "With her savings [of time and strength] she plants fruitful vines in her vineyard" (Proverbs 31:16). God has not only given you the responsibility to be your husband's helpmate, but your life is also about the fruit that is produced from what you plant. There is a saying that "we reap what we sow." As you recognize priorities and begin to live out your life according to God's order, you will begin to see the reward of your obedience.

The woman of virtue spends time planting vines that bear fruit. It is part of our responsibility to instill morals, discipline, value, responsibility, integrity, and self-worth into our children. See your children as the vineyard, and the characteristics you instill in them as the vines. The time you save from your outside distractions should now be redirected into time invested within your home with your husband and children. The fruitful vines are also the characteristics you display to your husband and children. They say the "apple doesn't fall far from the tree," so instilling values in your children is not just about dictation or orders of demand, it's about living out examples of the characteristics you want them to have. The Bible instructs for us to, "Train up a child in the way he should go and when he is old he will not depart from it" (Proverbs 22:6). In order for us to be able to plant vines that are fruitful, we ourselves must bear fruit.

Remember the story in the Bible about the fig tree found in Mark 11:12-14? Jesus, on the way from Bethany, was hungry when He saw a tree that was supposed to have fruit. Now, a fig tree is a tree that has beautiful leaves and under those leaves there is supposed to be fruit. From afar, the tree looks healthy and strong and enticing and, even better, at close range you are supposed to see the wonderful fruit that is covered by the leaves. But when Jesus approached this tree, He saw no fruit, and so He cursed the fig tree. Many times, as Christians, we are just like that fig tree. We appear enticing, well put together, beautiful and well-rounded, and all who look on the outside appearance are impressed. But, what about our roots, the close-up appearance, the parts that people cannot see from afar? What type of fruit are you bearing on your fig tree? Is there any at all?

When the people brought a complaint to Him about the Galileans, Jesus spoke to them about repenting of their sins, He never addressed their complaint. He instructed them to repent for their own sins. He then spoke a parable to them saying, "A certain man had a fig tree, planted in his vineyard, and he came looking for fruit on it, but did not find [any]" (Luke 13:6, AMP). Jesus was illustrating two points here. One was that while we are busy looking and complaining and criticizing and gossiping about others, we ought to worry about ourselves. Secondly, the fig tree we plant (our appearance) must bear the fruit of who we claim to be.

While diligently working towards being a better woman of God, you must be aware of the things that you need to improve. Also bear in mind that your husband and children are watching. How would you expect your husband and children to display characteristics of patience and forgiveness if you yourself are not patient or forgiving? Let's look at a bunch of grapes. First there is the stem, and from the stem are branches, and attached to the branches are the grapes. Woman of virtue, pretend that each grape is a demonstration of the type of fruit that you bear. See yourself as the tendril and your children as the vine (a vine is a stem that trails or creeps by winding itself about a support with tendrils). Tendrils attach themselves or entwine themselves as a support to the plant and act like anchors that help the plant to grow. I use this metaphor hoping you can clearly envision yourself as the tendril, a support for your children as they, like the vine, trail themselves, holding fast to their dependence on you. Live a life that they can see, and not one that they curse because the appearance is different from the reality. Your fig tree must bear the fruit of the spirit, which is love, joy, peace, forbearance, kindness, goodness, gentleness and self-control. And, as the tendril, you need to support your children by teaching them God's way in love and acting like an anchor so that as they grow they feel secure in your direction and guidance. It may not be evident right away, and it may seem as though your effort to grow your children in the right way is not working, but when seeds are planted, the end result takes a while to manifest. In due time, the seeds that were planted will bear fruit of their kind.

"She girds herself with strength [spiritual, mental, and physical fitness for her God-given task] and makes her arms strong and firm" (Proverbs 31:17, AMP).

Even as I write this book, God has shown me the importance of spiritual, mental, and physical strength. It's amazing how God can use you, even while He is still working on you. I encountered a challenge a few days prior to writing this part of the book, and at first I was reluctant to share it, but what better way to show God's changing power than to use real life examples and situations. I was confronted by a person who has always known how to bring out the worst in me. He decided to show up at my home one day unannounced, and as he stood at my doorstep it was obvious that he had come for a confrontation. As I quietly and calmly began addressing the nature of his visit, he became more aggressive in his tone and began to insult me and curse at me. At first, I maintained my composure, but then I began to feel warm inside, and shortly afterwards I lost all control of my emotions and began to shout and curse back at him as I replayed in my mind all the things he had ever done to hurt me in the past. Things got so intense that I felt like a grade school child ready to settle the score with a fight.

The next morning, as I began to prepare for my devotions, I sat on my living room floor and cried as I felt convicted in my spirit. I was hurt, I was frustrated, but, most of all, I was disappointed in myself and in my behaviour. I knelt down beside my couch and began to cry out to God, "I can't do this alone. I need to hear from you. I don't want to wait until tomorrow, I need you now!" I began to pray and ask God for forgiveness for how I had behaved the day before. When I finished praying, I tuned in to watch Joyce Meyer, and she was preaching a message titled "Power Gone Sour." She spoke about grieving the Holy Spirit and how when we grieve or sadden the Holy Spirit we begin to feel that grief, which was much of what I was feeling a few moments before. She explained that we can grieve the Holy Spirit by how we speak and the words that come out of our mouths. She then used a scriptural reference, "Let no foul or polluting language, nor evil word nor unwholesome or worthless talk [ever] come out of your mouth, but only such [speech] as is good and beneficial to the spiritual progress of others, as is fitting to the need and the occasion, that it may be a blessing and give grace (God's favour) to those who hear it!" (Ephesians 4:29, AMP).

I began to cry in repentance and found myself thinking, "Ugh! I failed! Why? Why did I let him get to me?

Okay, God, I get it!" Then to top it off, she talked about the fig tree and used the same scriptural references I used a few pages back in this book. She said that the reason Jesus cursed the fig tree was because it was a phoney. So, I chuckled because I felt like a child being scolded by a parent. I began to wonder if the neighbours had heard me. What example of a Christian woman would I have been?

So, there I was in the midst of writing this book about the woman of virtue and an opportunity of challenge came my way, and I blew it. I failed to gird myself with strength. To gird is to encircle a person or part of the body with a belt or band. The woman of virtue girds herself with strength. Had I encircled myself with spiritual strength that day, even though the visit was a surprise to me, there would have been nothing that he could do to allow me to grieve the Holy Spirit of God. Girding yourself is to always be prepared. Always be aware that it is important to encircle yourself with the strength of God's Word and, through prayer, prepare yourself for the unexpected things that may come up in your day. Living your life as a woman of virtue is not a ritual, it's a lifetime commitment to walk in accordance and obedience to the Word of God. Although we may fail at times, God is there to correct us and mold us into His image and likeness. Remember the rubies and pearls in Chapter 1? We must go through a process before reaching perfection.

Life can be challenging at times, and you may feel like you have everything under control, but it's when you are placed in the fire or put to the test that you see the truth about how much more work God has to do in you. Joyce Meyer also used the example of an orange that had been ripened under gas and looks beautiful in the store, but when we cut it open, it is a dried up mess. Her question was, "What happens when our fruit is squeezed?"

Woman of virtue, we must encircle ourselves with spiritual strength, recognizing that the enemy roams throughout the earth seeking whom he can devour. My husband and I love to watch the nature channels. It's amazing to see the instincts of the animals and how the predator seeks out the prey in order to catch it, particularly the tactics of the lions. It hides behind the bush, waiting for the prey to get within a certain distance for it to make its killing attack. Satan works in the very same way. He doesn't attack you when he knows you are on the alert, he catches you off guard. Much like a soldier out to war, we need to be prepared for the unknown. The soldier does not take off his armour because he anticipates his enemy's attack, and for that reason he is always prepared and armed.

It is essential to have a holistic approach when you are girded with strength. Although the spiritual aspect is the most important, it is also important to be physically and mentally secure. Do you realize that everything you do begins with your thought process? How you feel, what you believe, the choices you make, and who you become all begin with a thought, and through the thought decisions and choices are made which then become realities through the physical actions you take.

It wasn't until I began to feel disrespected and poorly treated by this person that I made the choice to react. Then, in that moment, I became a woman who did not display the characteristics of a woman of God.

Paul says, "Whatever things are true, noble, just, pure, lovely, of good report, meditate on these things" (Philippians 4:8). Satan loves to distract us with negative thoughts of anger, depression, fear, sadness, anxiety, bitterness, envy, hatred, and malice. But, the Bible says that we are to put those things away (Ephesians 4:31; 1 Peter 2:1; Colossians 3:8).

At times, our life circumstances and situations make it difficult to keep our focus on the Lord. It is so easy to fear or have anxiety about what we see, even though it's been tried, tested, and proven that Jesus Christ has always been faithful. The distractions of what we believe to be our reality in our current circumstances cause us to take our eyes off of the Lord. In Matthew 14:22-32, Jesus sent His disciples on a boat. This was after He had done the miracle of feeding thousands with the five loaves of bread and two fish. He left the disciples alone and went to pray, and the boat drifted off in the middle of the sea due to waves and winds that were contrary. Jesus appeared out on the water, but at first the disciples thought He was a ghost. Peter told Jesus to confirm it was Him by asking him to come out onto the water. Jesus called him to come, and Peter was able to walk on the water as he headed in the direction of Christ. But then Peter paid attention to the winds and began to fear. He began to sink and cried out for the Lord to help him. The

Bible says that Jesus *immediately* stretched out His hand and caught him. Then he said, "O you of little faith, why did you doubt?" (Matthew 14:31)

At times, we are just like Peter. A few hours prior to getting on the boat, they witnessed Jesus' ability to perform a miracle by feeding the five thousand. He took the little they had and fed many; they saw it for themselves, this wasn't hearsay. Jesus was out of their sight when He went to pray, and He left them alone with evidence of what He was capable of. Peter walked on water, and it was only when he began to look at the circumstances around him that he began to sink.

Many times, the circumstances around us are like the wind—our struggles, hurt, pain, financial issues, and relationship issues. We need to remember the times when Jesus gave us evidence of His existence in our lives, and avoid the sinking process. We can't allow our focus to be on what is occurring around us, forgetting the importance of focusing on Christ before us. The awesome thing I love about this story is that when Peter's focus shifted and he began to sink, the Bible says he cried out for Jesus's help, and Jesus *immediately* extended a helping hand. Even though Peter lost faith, Jesus was still willing to extend a helping hand. What an awesome thought. God understands that our circumstances are a distraction, but He is also here to say, "You are not alone. I am here."

Notice that Jesus went off to pray alone when He sent them on the boat. Couldn't it be possible that Jesus was interceding in prayer about the storm the very same way the Holy Spirit intercedes for us today? (Romans 8:26-28). Jesus said that when He is gone from this earth He would send the Holy Spirit to advocate on our behalf (John 16:7). At times, we are not sure how to pray about a situation or what to do about a certain decision or how to feel or how to react or what to believe. We are faced with many storms, conflicts, and contradictions in our lives, but we must, as women of virtue, gird ourselves with spiritual, mental, and physical fitness to withstand these storms. We must be confident and remember that Jesus is capable and available to carry us through if we keep our eyes on Him.

Physical fitness is important. Although your spirit may be fed and you may feel like you have your spiritual walk down pat, if the carrier or host of your spirit is weak and unfit, it's only a matter of time before it begins to affect the inner man. Once I began to get serious about looking at my Christian walk from a holistic approach, the Lord began to speak to me about taking care of my physical body. At first I thought, "Yeah, I know, I know!" but then, whenever I'd watch a Christian program, there would be more and more preachers speaking about taking care of the physical body. Was there a message here? I think so.

It may be far-fetched if you are someone who has never worked out a day in your life or if you are one with an eating habit that seems impossible to break, but there is hope. Take baby steps, if you feel that your physical body lacks energy and you know consciously that you probably should be eating healthier, take small steps to make life changes that will be beneficial to you in the long run. Try implementing healthier choices, try walking a few times a week, or try getting a workout DVD. It won't all change in one night, but make the effort to take care of the body you have; after all, remember that it is the only one you'll ever have, and you're stuck with it for life.

"She tastes and sees that her gain from work [with and for God] is good; her lamp goes not out, but it burns on continually through the night [of trouble, privation, or sorrow warning away fear, doubt, and mistrust]" (Proverbs 31:18, AMP).

What a rewarding feeling it would be to see the manifestations of your efforts to live a life that fulfills God's will for you as a woman of virtue. Living a life as a woman of virtue is undoubtedly difficult and, once again, this is not about perfection, it's about recognizing the value that God has placed on you, knowing who He has created you to be, and striving to continue to walk in His image of you.

Have you ever encountered a very difficult challenge? Something you struggled with but determined to complete because you desired to do so? Think of how rewarding it was when you met your goal, how proud you were that you never gave up. Living out your life as a woman of virtue is no different than any other goal you may have. It's challenging, but very possible. As you strive to live out a life that is pleasing to God, assessing and reassessing yourself must become second nature to you. Romans 8:1 says, "There is therefore now no condemnation to those who are in Christ Jesus, who do not walk according to the flesh, but according to the spirit." As a woman of God, your actions and behaviours should now be based on your spiritual walk, in all you do and in all you say make a conscious effort to assess if your actions are based on the flesh or on the spirit. Bear in mind that condemnation is for the actions of the flesh. As a woman of virtue, your obedience to walk in the spirit and not in the flesh is what will govern your spiritual walk with Christ. It is one thing to desire this change in your life, however it truly is an everyday walk and you have to be consistent in your ways, thinking, and behaviour. It is a lifestyle change and not one that will occur overnight, but one that will be rewarding.

There are times when I feel I have it all under control, and I am ready for any challenge that life can throw at me, but it is only when the trials come unexpectedly and catch me off guard that reality hits, and I realize I still have a far way to go. It is in my trials that the Holy Spirit opens my eyes to areas of weakness and the things I need to continue to work on to become a better woman of God. James spoke to the early church and told them to count it all joy when they fall into diverse temptations. He told them that the temptation was a test of faith that would produce patience and that patience would create perfection within them. James emphasised the importance of not being double-minded, and referred to a double-minded man as being a wave of the sea driven and tossed by the wind. He assured them that such a man would receive nothing from God because he was unstable. James was precise in what he said, but he also challenged them to seek God if they lacked wisdom (James 1:2-8).

As a woman of virtue, there is a lot that you can take from this scripture. Firstly, realize that when God allows you to be tempted in any area of your life, He is not playing games with you. Your character can only be developed under testing in that very same area. For example, if you have a weakness in patience and require and desire to change in that area, guess what? God's going to allow some trials to come in your path so you can develop the character of patience. If you have a weakness to anger and need to work on self-control or managing your mouth and the way you talk to and about others, guess what? God will allow some challenges to come your way to develop a spirit of humility and self-control.

You may not realize it but the building of your character works very much like the things you do in your everyday life. If you want to learn something, it is a step-by-step process. You gather the information required, you learn how it needs to be done, and then you test it. You do it in school when you are taught the curriculum and then you are tested to see how well you have learned. If you want to bake or cook, you obtain the ingredients and learn how it is done, and then you test it by actually doing what you have learned. The Bible says that God does not tempt us because He himself cannot be tempted (James 1:13). God does, however, allow these temptations in our lives so that He can shape us into the people He desires us to be. Anything we endure in life helps us to develop, and this development is needed in order to help build character.

It's like a person who is dedicated to building muscles at the gym. Anyone who has done a day of weightlifting or toning exercises at a gym will tell you that their muscles are sore and painful when they come from an intense workout, but with determination and dedication, they soon begin to see the physical evidence of their hard work. The muscles become firm and formed with definition in that muscle group, and there is no question that that individual has been doing some hard work to make a change in his or her appearance. Your walk as a woman of virtue is no different. Sure, there will be pain and struggles, you will be stretched and pushed, tested and tried, but on the other side of all of it, your gain from working with and for God will be good, and it will be evident. You and others will see the physical evidence of the time you have invested to become a better woman of God. What an exciting thought.

The biggest challenge you will find is the challenge of determination. Be determined and, no matter what, never give up. I can remember many times in my Christian walk feeling and thinking that this was just too hard. "I am never going to be able to do this!" I thought.

It felt like as soon as I had conquered one area of my life that there was something around the corner waiting on me. I can remember many times asking God to give me a break. I would literally pray and say, "God, I am not asking for you to take it all away, all I want is a break, I am so tired." I was frustrated. I felt very overwhelmed at times by the trials that kept coming my way. Although I felt this way, I was comforted by the still voice of the Lord reassuring me that "troubles don't last always, joy comes in the morning," and "after the rain comes sunshine." I had to learn to not allow the spirit of defeat to dictate my life.

I believe that when the Scripture says that "Her lamp goes not out but it burns on continually through the night," it means just that. No matter how you feel, no matter how frustrating it may seem, and no matter how many times a trial comes your way, keep pushing. Press on towards the mark, keep on praying, keep on changing, keep on keeping on. Never, ever give up!

If you have ever lit a candle you will notice that the moment you ignite it, the flame is bright and high. After it has been burning for a while the flame becomes dim, but notice that as long as there is still some candle wick left, that fire will keep on burning until you blow it out. See yourself as that candle. You may find that some days it feels like you've been burning for a long time (frustrated, weary, troubled, fearful, anxious, tired), you may even feel like there is no more candle left, and the flame may not be burning as brightly as when you were first lit, but as long as you don't blow out the flame (give up hope, quit, lose faith in God), you will keep on burning. God will never leave you alone.

While you go through the process, it's not always clear where your efforts will take you, but keep pursuing your goal with great expectations that the gains from your work will be good.

CHAPTER 6

"She stretches out her hands to the distaff, and her hand holds the spindle." (Proverbs 31:19)

When used as a noun, a distaff is a tool used in spinning. It is made to hold the unspun fibres and keep the fibres from tangling, making the spinning process easier. When used as an adjective, distaff refers to the female's side of the family. In the communities where a distaff was used, it symbolized domestic life. A spindle is used in conjunction with a distaff. It is a straight spike that is usually made out of wood, and it is used for spinning. The distaff holds the unspun fibres and the spindle spins to neatly bring the fibres together.

As you are faced with daily tasks, life challenges, and situations, it may all seem like a tangled web with so many things to organize, so many tasks to complete and so many decisions to make. If you are anything like me, at times I just want to know where to begin. Picture every area of your life like a string of fibre, without that distaff and spindle you would have one big tangled mess. If we do not learn the importance of sorting out and organizing the priorities in our lives, that is exactly what we will find—one big tangled mess.

Referring back to the distaff as a symbol of domestic life, our responsibility, as women of virtue, first lies in our households. I remember many times coming home after a long day at work and finding that dinner had not yet been put on the stove, the children were nowhere near ready for bed, homework had not been done, and it felt like I only had a few hours before morning came again. I sometimes worked fourteen days straight, and my husband worked over ten hours most of the time as well. My priorities were not in alignment with the Word of God. It was no wonder I often felt overwhelmed. I didn't have much time for anything, nevermind a list of things that I needed to do in the house. The affairs of my household were far from my first priority. Although, I must say, I felt like I was doing the right thing by working to help keep a roof over my family's head and put food on the table. I was doing what I was supposed to do, or so I thought.

The more I was not in alignment with my role as a wife and a mother, the more miserable I became. I began to see my children growing up very quickly with not much memory of how they reached there so fast. Many times after getting paid, I would think, "Is this what I am spending my time away from my obligations doing? Is it really worth it?" Although the answer was "No," I kept on going, thinking that I was doing what I had to do. Now I am not implying that as a woman of virtue you cannot work outside of your home, but what I am saying is that if the job you're doing is interfering with the priorities you should be fulfilling within your household, then maybe it is time to reassess.

I decided to include a picture of a woman grasping the spindle and guiding the fibres from the distaff because when I saw it the picture illustrated something important to me. As this woman holds the distaff on her shoulder, she guides the fibres and spins it with control. The spindle holds these fibres neatly together, and everything is in place. Whatever struggles or challenges you are facing at this present time in your life, picture them for a minute. The distaff over your shoulder is the heavy load that you are carrying. Whatever the circumstances are, *you* have the ability to guide your situation and take control of it. God is the spindle that holds the fibres of your life together, but you have to be willing to direct your situation to Him, and with your efforts to do so, it will all come together.

Being a wife, mother, and a woman who works outside of the home has posed many challenges for me throughout the years. It wasn't until I began to read and study about the woman of virtue and prayed about it that God began to open my eyes to see that the virtuous woman is one who is well organized and who puts a lot of thought into her actions and decisions before and when she makes them. She is one who takes time to carefully look into her life and see how her decisions affect her and the ones around her. It is no question that she understands her God-given role, and she makes every effort to take care of her family and household. To be a woman of virtue, you must know your role and value as given by God. You are unique and specially made by God, and there is a purpose for you.

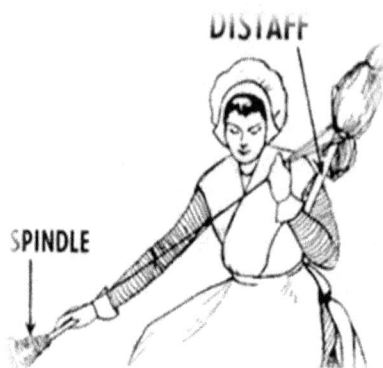

The task of finding a balance in life may seem difficult and even impossible at times. I can remember thinking many times, "God, you made me a helper, not a slave." Sometimes I would be so frustrated it would bring me to tears. I was in a rush much of the time. Rushing to work, rushing to get home, rushing to do dinner, rushing to get the kids bathed and in bed, there was just not enough time. I was overwhelmed, frustrated, and tired. I never stopped to think that maybe, just maybe, I needed to *stop*

and spend some time with my husband and children that God had so graciously blessed me with.

You see, Satan has a way of bombarding us with all kinds of emotions and thoughts. His plan is to confuse us, upset us, and frustrate us to the point where we feel like giving up. I can remember while praying for God to transform me into a woman of virtue that there were times when I felt it was never going to happen. At times, when I struggled, I felt very alone, not even my husband understood. As I tried to balance things between my work life and home life, it seemed to become more and more difficult. I felt like God was trying to show me that my priorities were not in place. My unspun fibres were my issues with finding the right balance between my work life and home life. It was one of the many struggles that I had, but this one particularly challenged me as God began to open my eyes to this woman of virtue, a woman I was eager to be like. God began to show me that everything I desired was very possible, but I would have to make some changes to the way I did things. Even now, as I write, God is still working in me.

We have to make up in our mind that change is necessary. We have to recognize that our role, as God created it, is supposed to be lived out throughout our lives. I truly believe that a lot of marriages break down because we neglect to do things the way God has ordered us to do them, and oftentimes we do not fulfill the role that God designed for us to fulfill. It would take a whole other book to really elaborate on that statement but, in essence, God loves order. He placed man as the head of the home for leadership and woman as the helper for partnership. How many married couples can sincerely say, in this day and age, that their home is in order the way God instructed it to be?

If you are reading this book and you are single, this still applies to you. What better way to prepare for your role as a man's future wife? After all, Proverbs 31 is based on a mother's advice to her son as to what to look for in a woman. You may not have the same unspun fibres as the woman who is married, but as a single woman there are many issues in life that could easily spin out of control in some of the same areas as those who are married. You could be struggling with finances, being mixed up in the wrong types of relationships, fornication, struggling with loneliness, frustrated with decision-making, whatever it is it still requires the process of guidance and direction (the distaff to the spindle). Woman of virtue, don't allow your circumstances to get the best of you. Life can become chaotic and disorderly at times, circumstances can change, situations that are unexpected can invite themselves into your life, and things can spin out of control. Grab hold of those loose fibres of your life and hold them together. You may not know how it will all be sorted out, but if you just grab a hold of it and give it to God, He can be the spindle of your life that takes those loose fibres and neatly puts them all together. God sees the end product of those pieces of unspun fibres, and He is the one who will produce the end result.

"She opens her hand to the poor, yes, she reaches out her filled hands to the needy [whether in body, mind, or spirit]." (Proverbs 31:20, AMP)

We can be so wrapped up in our own circumstances and situations that we fail to consider those who are worse off than we are. We can be so selfish and self-centred that all we care about is what is transpiring in our own lives. We neglect to see that someone around us may be suffering just as badly as, or worse, than we are. So, why would extending a hand to the poor or reaching out to the needy be relevant to a woman of virtue? It's not that difficult to see that God wants us to take the focus off ourselves. God is the most unselfish being, and part of being a woman of virtue is to be unselfish, too. If you are a mother and a wife, you are probably thinking, "How much more unselfish can I be?" Well, wait a minute. That's why you are extending a hand. Part of being a woman of virtue is to go beyond the four walls of your home, and reach out to others in the world that are hurting or suffering in some way. God is willing to use you to bless those around you, if you allow Him to.

The woman of virtue opens her filled hands to the needy. Note that your hands don't need to be filled with material things like money. Knowledge and encouragement can be just as helpful, if not more so, to someone who is discouraged or feeling low. As a woman of virtue, a great habit to develop is that of giving. Giving to others in need can be either financial or emotional.

While it is true that your family is your first priority, recognizing the needs of others allows God to display His love through you to others. You develop that 'love your neighbour as yourself' characteristic with a clear perception of what that means as you live it out in your own life. I can remember many times in my life when I was going through difficult times that God would present me with an opportunity to bless someone financially or emotionally, and the expression of gratitude from those individuals would give me a feeling of purpose. I knew that even when I was struggling in certain areas of my own life that God could and wanted to use me to extend a hand to someone in need.

Look at the story in Matthew 19:16-24. Here was a man who asked Jesus what he should do in order to possess eternal life. He was certain he had followed all of the commandments, but he was still curious to know if he lacked anything. Jesus responded to him by telling him to sell what he owned and follow Him. When the man heard this he turned away because the thought of selling all he had to follow Jesus was stressful to him. I am not convinced that Jesus would have expected him to give up all of his possessions; more than likely, it was the reply of willingness that Jesus was looking for. Was this man who claimed that he had followed the commandments from his youth capable of giving away what he had? Was he willing to sacrifice his possessions to help the needy? Was he able to let go of the things he possessed in order to lend a helping hand to another? Jesus offered him something far greater than earthly treasures, He offered him heavenly treasures, but because the man could not see that which Christ had to offer, he rejected it for the things that he had placed great value on here on Earth.

Look at how Jesus responded after the man walked away (Matthew 19:23-24), "Truly I say, it will be difficult for a rich man to enter into the kingdom of heaven, and again I say to you, it is easier for a camel to go through the eye of a needle than for a rich man to go into the kingdom of heaven." The message here is to put the needs of others before your own. Jesus had told the man to take what he had and give it to those in need and then follow Him. Jesus was about putting the needs of others before His own. He was about giving and sharing, loving and helping others.

The woman of virtue is one that has moral standards, and part of that is to seek out those who are hurting and those who are in need. What do you have to sell and give to the poor, woman of virtue? Is there someone you could sacrifice a possession of yours to help? Is there someone you could sacrifice a day of your busy schedule to pray for? Is there someone who could use an encouraging word from you? Is there someone who needs you? Virtuous woman, sell what you have, give your time, your possessions, your love, your help, your encouraging words to those in need, and follow Jesus!

Jesus has much more to offer you than what you can see on Earth. I think we forget that all the things we possess on Earth are left behind once we have passed on. The most precious possession you can possess is that of eternal life. When you make the decision to lend a helping hand, it is not so that you can present yourself in a self-righteous way, it is not to receive praise from others, or so you can feel good about yourself. You are to display Christ, so that those around you who do not know Christ will see His light in you. Look at what Christ says in Matthew 6:1-2, "Take heed that you do not do your charitable deeds before men, to be seen by them. Otherwise you have no reward from your father in heaven, therefore when you do a charitable deed, do not sound a trumpet before you as the hypocrites do in the synagogues and in the streets, that they may have glory from men. Assuredly, I say to you, they have their reward." Jesus instructed that we shouldn't even let our left hand know what our right hand is doing. He emphasized being humble and putting away the urge to boast. You are not doing these things to receive glory from others; you do these things to the glory of God. Recognize that, as a woman of virtue, God has given you the ability to extend a hand to those who are in need.

As we live out our lives on Earth, we must live on purpose, with purpose. We can become overwhelmingly preoccupied with wanting to possess earthly treasures and miss our calling. We were made by God, not to obtain material things on earth, but to do His will on Earth. This is not to say that we should not obtain material things while we are on Earth, but the Bible says that where our treasure is, there our hearts will be also. The man's treasure was in his possessions, and his heart was also there. He displayed this when he rejected giving his possessions away to the poor. God may place you in a situation to give to someone in need, but reluctance can take over because you fear that if you give what you have, you yourself may end up lacking. You may have your last bit of money and see that someone is in need of money, but you think to yourself, "If I give this away, what will I have for myself?" Or you may have a possession of some sort and you see that someone may have better use for it than you do, but you think to yourself, "If I give this to them, then what do I do without it?" Here is what God thinks about an attitude that is reluctant to give. "Do not lay up for yourselves treasures on earth, where moth and rust destroy and where thieves break in and steal; but lay up for yourselves treasures in heaven, where neither moth nor rust destroy and where thieves do not break in and steal"(Matthew 6:19-20). Earthly things are for a time only; the things you possess will come and go. Internal treasures are the things that cannot be taken away or destroyed.

There is a feeling of warmth and fulfilment in giving to someone in need. While someone is waiting for a miracle from God to supply a need, you might just be the one God wants to use to help fulfill that need. Open your heart and mind, pray and ask God how you, woman of virtue, can open your hands to someone in need. If you find yourself reluctant to give because you have needs of your own, give by faith believing that God will supply and fulfill the things that you lack, and watch God do the impossible in your life.

CHAPTER 7

⁂

*"She fears not the snow for her family, for all
her household are doubly clothed in scarlet."
(Proverbs 31:21, AMP)*

Scarlet is a bright red colour with a tinge of orange. The colour orange represents the energy of red and the happiness of yellow. It is affiliated with joy, success, encouragement, happiness, and determination. Symbolically, the covering of scarlet can refer to the shed blood of Jesus Christ. The virtuous woman has no fear for her family because all of her household is doubly clothed in scarlet. She has ensured that her household is covered by the blood of Jesus Christ. She is a woman of prayer!

I understand fully what it is to have fear and anxiety

concerning family. As women, we naturally worry over the well-being of our children, our husbands, and our household. We want to nourish and protect, and we become nervous if we don't have control over a particular situation. I remember finding out about my first pregnancy. I was excited. I was about to become a mother, what a joyful feeling that was. After having my first child and watching her grow, I had anxiety over many things, such as the first time she had to walk alone to school, sending her in an elevator, her taking the bus alone, and as I had more children, I had the same feelings with each of them. When they were sick, I worried; when they were sleeping, I had to check in to make sure they were still breathing; when they were at school, I wanted to be sure the other children treated them right; when they were out of the home, I couldn't wait for them to come back so I knew they were okay. In the very same way, I felt anxiety over the life and well-being of my husband. I was nervous if he wasn't home on time; I wondered if he was alright. I can go on and on about the anxiety I had concerning my family. And when they were not around me, I felt I could not protect them. The truth is their lives were not in my hands to protect, they were in the hands of God all along. My responsibility was to do what I could do and control the things I could control, like taking care of my household and loving my husband and children. My responsibility was to pray for them and over every situation I had no control over. The Bible says that the prayer of a righteous person avails much (James 5:16). Whether it is the health and strength, financial, emotional, spiritual, or physical well-being of your family, you can cover all grounds through prayer.

Winter is my least favourite time of the year. I hate the feeling of cold weather. And although the snow is beautiful to look at when it falls and sits nicely on the trees, grass, or mountains, it is a terror to drive in snowy weather conditions. I can remember the first time I spun out on a snowy day. I saw my life flash before my eyes as I held on tightly to the steering wheel and watch the car spin out of control. No matter how hard I tried to gain control over that car, there was nothing I could do to make the car stop when I wanted it to. There might be many uncontrollable situations in your life, and just like that spinning car, you may want to take control of them, but sometimes there are situations that you will not be able to control.

There is a song I love to listen to called "Jesus Take the Wheel," sung by Carrie Underwood. The analogy in this song is amazing as it speaks about a woman driving her car as she goes through challenges in her personal life. As she is driving, she loses control of the car and sees her life flashing before her eyes. She then comes to the recognition that she has no control over her physical life. She starts to pray for Jesus to take the wheel. She needed God to take control of her life, both at that moment and overall. She realized that she couldn't do it on her own, so she resorted to prayer. Here is a woman who has lost control in her life, and she's in a car which she has no control over. God had to show her, using the situation she was in at that very moment, how

96

powerless she was. It wasn't until she began to pray, first recognizing the inability to do things on her own, that the car came to a stop. She decided that from that day on she was going to give the wheel of her life over to Christ for direction, guidance, and protection.

At times in life, there are battles we may face, and some may be too much to handle. Life can seem like that uncontrollable car as the challenges keep coming. You may feel like there is no way to spin your life back in control. Give the wheel of your life over to Jesus Christ. Recognize that you can't do it on your own and that you don't have to. Jesus is more than willing to take the wheel of your life and steer it into the right direction. Cover your situation and your circumstances, cover your husband and your children, cover yourself and your finances, cover your health and emotions, cover your home and those who enter in it, cover your whole life with scarlet. Let the blood of Jesus Christ be a covering over everything.

The scarlet was the protection for the woman of virtue and her household, this is why she did not fear the snow for her family. She was confident that the covering of Christ Jesus was all she required to ensure that her family was protected and doubly clothed. When I was a child and had to wait outside for the school bus during the winter, I hated having to bundle up with the scarf, the hat, the gloves, and the ear muffs. All that gear was required to ensure that I was ready for the snowy weather. The first time I left home without my gloves and hat and decided I was too cool for boots, boy, did I pay severely for it. I never understood what frostbite was until that day. In the very same way we can sometimes fail to recognize the importance of our covering, and it is not until something bites us that we quickly realize our need for the Saviour.

It is important, woman of virtue, to prepare your household for all types of weather. It may seem like your life is sunshine today, but don't be over-confident and leave without that umbrella because when you least expect it you might be hit with a rain storm. I'm not suggesting you fear the worst, but be prepared by anchoring your life on the foundation of Christ. Whether you are living in your good times or in your bad times, always be prayerful and watchful over your household. In doing this, you have no reason to fear the snow because your household is doubly clothed in scarlet and, no matter what the weather is, you will be prepared for it.

When I think of 'doubly clothed' I see those days when the cold was so bitter that it was necessary to wear underclothing, double socks, and then the outerwear. Being doubly clothed meant we were well-prepared for the weather awaiting us, and because we were dressed so well, we knew we would be protected from the cold. I love the amplified version of doubly clothed because I see this as a double portion of protection. There is the spiritual aspect and the physical aspect of the covering. Not only are we able to pray for protection over our families and that the Spirit of God will abide with our household, the covering is for their spiritual well-being also. And if scarlet is associated with joy, success, encouragement, happiness, and determination, we have done well in clothing our household in a double layer of scarlet.

As women of virtue, not only should we stand firm in prayer over the well-being of our household, but we should also be set apart from the average. We must act different and live different, be honorable in character and stand as a vessel of encouragement. "Therefore, if anyone cleanses himself from what is dishonorable, he will be a vessel for honorable use, set apart as holy, useful to the master of the house, ready for every good work." (2 Timothy 2:21, ESV)

Are you one who prays, but your presence does not reflect a woman of faith? In Paul's letter to Timothy, he expresses the importance of not focussing on the minor things and arguments that might turn people away from getting the true meaning of the teachings of the gospel. He goes on to encourage him to be kind, mild tempered, and patient, and instructs him to approach opposition with gentleness in the hope that God would be the one to bring them to repentance for their wrongdoings.

While the woman of virtue is prayerful over her household, that doesn't mean that all will go well within her household at all times. The enemy is still real, and prayer will not exempt you or your family from his attacks. You may desire to live your life out as a woman of virtue but find that the harder you try to develop these characteristics the more challenging things become. You may be the only one in your household who is prayerful, who sees the importance of living out a life of moral righteousness before God. Your husband may not be a believer in Christ, and your children may have a hard time grasping the concept and beliefs of Christianity. Are your efforts in living a life as a woman of virtue then meaningless? No! God has a purpose for you, in the midst of all of this there is a reason He chose you to have a desire to live your life as a woman of virtue. As frustrating as it may be, if you are the only believer in your home, know that God wants to use you as a vessel of encouragement for your family and others around you.

When I became serious about my walk with Christ and God began to open my eyes, I wanted everyone in my household to see things the way God had revealed them to me. It was the most frustrating thing ever to see that I was the only one God had "revealed" things to. I was frustrated because my husband never prayed as much as I did, he never fasted when I did, and he wasn't reading the Word as much as I did. I felt like I was in a marriage but battling the enemy on my own, yet this was my husband's "job." Then there were the children; I wanted them to desire a relationship with God. How was I going to make them serve the Lord and get them to recognize their need for the Saviour?

As I became more and more frustrated, God revealed to me that this was *not* my job. It wasn't my job to bring my family under submission to God. We all have to stand before God and give an account for our own salvation. It wasn't my place to say how their relationships should be and what they needed to do in order to have one. Every relationship with God is between God and that individual. My responsibility was to pray that God would visit each one of them and reveal Himself to them and that they would be receptive to God and yield to the Lord in submission. How they came to God was not supposed to be my concern. My concern was to be a vessel of encouragement and an example of a Christian that they could see. Instead of being frustrated with my family for not changing with me, I learned to be mild-tempered and patient, waiting for God's hand to move as I prayed.

God wants you, as a woman of virtue, to be an encourager. Encourage your husband, be a wife of support. Encourage your children—encourage them in their academics, in their extracurricular activities, in their sports, and in their spiritual walk. Be easy to talk to and be understanding. Pray about how to approach the tough topics and what to do in times of controversy. Double clothing your household in scarlet means covering every aspect of your family's well-being, both physically and spiritually. There is no fear for the snow if you are geared up with all the right types and amounts of clothing for the cold weather. You will enjoy the snow much more if you don't have to worry about getting frostbite because you left your mittens!

"She makes tapestry for herself; her clothing is fine linen and purple." (Proverbs 31:22)

Tapestry is a form of textile (cloth or fabric) that is woven. It can be hung on the walls or used to cover furniture. I think it's fair to say that most women are the interior designers in their household, and decisions about wall colour and furniture are probably some of the decorative decisions we would make. Tapestry was not just used as a decorative piece for the wall or furniture, it had a more important function than that. It was used to insulate the walls of the castles back then. As we know, insulation is very important as this helps to protect the house from extreme weather, such as heat and cold. All along in Proverbs 31 the virtuous woman thinks only about her family, and then we get to Proverbs 31:22 and she finally thinks about herself. Or does she?

Let's go one step further and look at the word insulate. To insulate is to cover, line, or separate with a material that prevents or reduces the passage or transfer of heat, sound, or electricity; in other words, to insulate means to cover, wrap, or envelop. So, here we see that the woman of virtue makes her own insulation. She is covered, wrapped, and enveloped, but in what way is she insulated? What is she being protected from? As a woman of virtue, it is not only important to recognize the needs of your family and to cover your family with scarlet, you also need to be covered. If the covering of Christ is not over your life, then how effective will you be in your role within your family?

As a woman of virtue, it is important to acknowledge the need to be covered, wrapped, and enveloped in Christ's protection over your life. Every aspect of your life needs to be protected, covered, and insulated against the plan of the enemy. Satan is like the bitter cold trying to seep his way into your home and your life, but the insulation of Christ is all you need to keep him out. You will face many challenges in your walk with Christ, no doubt, but it's not about the challenges you face, it is how you go through these trials that matter. You need to prepare yourself on a daily basis by putting on the full armour of God for protection (Ephesians 6:11-18). God is faithful to those who depend on Him. The biggest mistake you can make is to feel like you are self-sufficient. God honours humility and a heart that is submissive to Him.

Look at the woman with the issue of blood in Luke 8:43. Here was a woman who suffered with an issue for years, she spent a lot of money going to physicians to obtain a diagnosis and a cure for her problem, but no one was able to help her. She then turned to Christ with the hope that He could help, but it didn't just stop with her hoping Jesus would be the solution to her problem. She made an effort to push through a crowd of people to get to Him. She knew and made up in her mind that all she needed to do was touch the fringe of his garment. She was confident that even just the tail end of His clothing was all she required for Him to make the impact and change in her life that she had been waiting for. It didn't stop there. Notice as Jesus moved through this great crowd of people that He felt that someone needed Him, and even when His disciples tried to convince Him that He was just feeling the brush of those passing by, He was certain that it was more than that. He knew there was a need for Him. It took the woman to then confess that she needed Him, and it was at that moment that He acknowledged her. He says in Luke 8:48 (AMP), "Daughter, your faith (your confidence and trust in Me) has made you well!" I love that Jesus addressed her on a personal level. He didn't call her woman, or lady, or ma'am, He said "Daughter." Jesus was addressing her as one of His own, and at that moment He reassured her that all was going to be well with her.

Becoming a woman of virtue is not an overnight transition; it will take time and a lot of effort. You may be going through a rough time right now, and if not now, then a time may come in the future, but whatever your situation is keep looking to God, keep pushing forward and striving to be and do your best. If there is a hardship that you are facing, keep hope and faith alive and remember that Jesus knows you by name. He is sensitive to your every need and desire. If you are like that woman with the issue of blood, reach out and touch the fringe of His garment and have faith that He can make you whole. Make yourself that tapestry for protection through daily prayer, asking God for new mercy every day, asking for His covering over your life, asking for guidance and the ability to live out your life according to His will and purpose for you. Allow God to be your insulation against the forces of darkness and the plans that the enemy has for you. In order for you to be that vessel of encouragement and that example for your family, you need to know the importance of praying for yourself.

"Her clothing is fine linen and purple" (Proverbs 31:22). They say that purple is the colour of royalty. Hold yourself in high esteem; you are part of the lineage of Christ. As a Christian, you are a representative of the Father. Although tapestry was made to insulate the castle walls, the appearance was attractive and of great quality. Pride yourself in being a woman of virtue. Your physical appearance is just as important as your inner self. Now, I'm not talking about vanity. How you conduct and present yourself as a woman of virtue should be a clear and true reflection of who you are inside and out. Make a conscious effort to put yourself together, look your best, smile your best, and remember who you are in Christ. Be confident in your inner and outer beauty. You may not always feel like it, but you will be surprised if you go against those feelings that your feelings will tend to follow your lead.

Attitude is also a reflection of who you are. Remember that fig tree? What you say, how you say it, what you do, and how you do it are all important things to be mindful of, and when and if you catch yourself being out of alignment with what you know God would expect of you, it is your responsibility to make it right. The clothing being fine linen and purple is not just about the outerwear; royalty must conduct themselves as people of great value on the inside as well.

"Her husband is known in the gates, when he sits among the elders of the land."
(Proverbs 31:23, ESV)

Make a conscious effort to speak highly of your husband. The way you talk and honour him among others says a lot about who you are as his wife. As women, we all know how we can become when we are upset or disappointed in our husbands. It is so easy to magnify all the things that we believe are wrong with them rather than embrace the things that are right. Make a conscious effort to honour your husband, not just with the respect you show him to his face, but also with how you speak about him to others. If you find yourself feeling or talking more negatively than positively about your husband, it's time to start praying for change. As you pray, ask God to change you and the way you deal with the issues you have with your spouse. Then begin to pray about the areas that you feel your husband needs to change. In the meantime, don't waste time trying to make him change through your efforts, chances are you will only frustrate yourself.

There is something about the elders. They are the best people to learn from and rub shoulders with because they bring wisdom and experience. I found over the years that whenever I struggled in an area, prayer came first, followed by seeking advice from those who have been there and done that. It was rewarding to hear godly wisdom from my elders and also have them align themselves with me in prayer.

It says a lot about a husband that is known in the gates when he sits among the elders. It's not so much that he is known but what is known about him. Are you one who gossips about your spouse? Do you put him down every chance you get? Are you uplifting him and honouring him with your words, or dishonouring him? Is he known in the gates as the love of your life, or as one whom you can't stand to be around? This may seem far-fetched to some of you, but I can assure you that there are women out there who have displayed little respect for their husbands by the way they speak about them publicly.

A woman of virtue displays the respect she has for her husband by how she speaks about him to others. How you characterize your husband is how others will view him. If you are having issues with your husband, the answer is not to speak negatively about him to others. In a humble and loving way make a request to the elders to pray for the both of you.

"Let the elders that rule well be counted worthy of double honour, especially those who labour in the word and doctrine" (1 Timothy 5:17). It is always a good idea to find an honourable, worthy, and dedicated elder woman or man of God to mentor you through your walk with Christ, someone who is not judgemental and is always willing to pray with and for you without delay. There will be times when they will be needed, trust me in this.

As a woman of virtue, this walk is not one you can

do on your own, some of the challenges you may face will require guidance from someone with a little more experience than you have. Whether it is issues within yourself, within your marriage, or with your children, the elders have the privilege of experience and wisdom that you can benefit from.

A woman of virtue should always be willing to learn from those who have experienced life. Learning from the elders does not always need to be due to a problem, it could be learning things like cooking a meal or baking, or tips on keeping a home with structure and cleanliness, it could be learning how to fast and pray, or how to live a balanced life as a Christian and how to deal with life challenges. I am not implying that the elders have it all figured out or have the answers to all your questions or problems, but I am saying that with the elders come wisdom, and if they labour in the word and doctrine they are equipped to give you sound advice.

Woman of virtue, if you are ever tempted to trash talk your husband to others, choose the alternative and let your husband be known in the gates and among the elders of the land in a positive, uplifting, and honourable way. If you are having concerns or troubles, find the elders who can give you advice and who can pray for and with you. As you do this, you also honour God.

CHAPTER 8

"She makes fine linen garments and leads others to buy them; she delivers to the merchants girdles [or sashes that free one up for service]."
(Proverbs 31:24, AMP)

Not only does the woman of virtue seek advice from the elders who have had more experience than she has, but she also serves as an elder to those who are younger than she is. She offers advice and wisdom from her experiences, and she is available and willing to mentor, pray for, and be an example to the younger generations to follow.

Back in Chapter 3, I spoke about the fruit of flax being a round, dry capsule containing several seeds.

Coincidentally, linen is made from the fibres of flax plants, and linen is of great value. If the woman of virtue makes fine linen and leads others to buy them, then these seeds that she is leading others to buy (aquire, obtain, get) are of great quality and value. Woman of virtue, making fine linen garments and leading others to buy them is simply what you have to offer that will help others grow and add value to their lives. The things you have learned in your life can be an encouragement, guidance, or source of knowledge for those who haven't been where you are as yet.

As we grow in Christ, we develop from babes to mature Christians, and along the way seeds are planted that eventually grow and mature. In your maturity you can begin to sow those seeds into the lives of others. Leading others is part of your job, woman of virtue. Allow the Lord to show you where and how to plant seeds in the people around you. Make your fine linen garments by the way you represent Christ in your own life. Lead by way of example, be prepared to offer words of encouragement, be willing to pray for others, and be ready to lead others to buy that fine linen, which is the way to Christ Jesus.

A sash is a large and colourful ribbon or band of material worn around the body. The virtuous woman supplies sashes for the merchants. While it is one thing to lead people to buy, people are usually reluctant to buy something unless the one telling them to buy it has made the purchase themselves. As you lead others in the way of Christ, they may be faced with challenges or situations that you can't fix or that you may not have the answers to. It is not for you to lead them by your words only, but to pray for them and be a source of intervention through your prayers. Your prayers for someone may be a shield of protection and a band of security. The power of prayer can open the spiritual eyes of the spiritually blind. Prayer can bring a prodigal back to his family, heal a broken marriage, or break the bondage that someone has been struggling with. Prayer can cover many situations and is the answer and solution to all problems and concerns. As you make linen garments and sell them, it's your duty to obtain that which you are selling. As you lead others to buy, cover them with the power of prayer. You are the representation of fine linen.

"Strength and dignity are her clothing and her position is strong and secure; she rejoices over the future [the latter day or time to come, knowing that she and her family are in readiness for it]!" (Proverbs 31:25, AMP)

It is said that you can tell a lot about a person by their attire and the way they carry themselves. While the outer appearance can be deceiving, it is usually a good indication of the type of individual a person is. You can perceive someone who dresses with confidence and pride, one who has good self-esteem and self-worth, and I think it's fair to say that the same could be said for someone who may be insecure or lack self-esteem and confidence. The woman of virtue has strength and dignity as her attire. Wow, what an appearance!

Strength—the ability to resist being moved or broken by a force; strong, able to withstand great force or pressure.

Clothes are items worn to cover the body, so the woman of virtue is covered with the ability to resist being moved or broken by a force. She is clothed with the ability to withstand great force or pressure. In the beginning of the book, I spoke about the value that God places on us, even when we are in our beginning phases like the rubies and jewels. You may have come from a past that has made you feel worthless or of no value, a past that looks very much like that dirty oyster. There might have been a time when the clothing you wore was of guilt and shame. The enemy set a plan in place for you, and had it not been for God imagine where you would be. The woman of virtue was not born with the clothing of strength and dignity, she had to go through the process of strength training and earn it.

Strength training is one of the most difficult activities, especially for those who have never worked out a muscle group in their lives. I remember the first time I ever tried strength training, I paid for it the next morning. I was so sore, and every muscle I had felt like a bag of weights was tied to them. My legs were heavy, and my arms were sore. However, the more I pushed myself, the easier the strength training seemed to become. It seemed easier because my muscles were being conditioned to what I was doing with regular practice. Muscle works by memory, so as I continued to train, the more my muscles adjusted because they had been trained to endure.

The past you lived through was the strength training for your present and future. When God is setting you up for greater, He has to bring you through a period of uncomfortable strength training. He needs to develop your spiritual muscles so you can withstand the forces of your opposition, Satan. Woman of virtue, as you look back into your past and see where God has taken you from, clap your hands with joy. Recognize that God has stripped you of that raggedy clothing and robed you in His love and forgiveness, attire that you can be proud of.

You are that woman of strength and dignity. You are an ambassador of a loving and forgiving God. The woman of virtue is clothed in strength and dignity because she went through the process of strength training. She endured, she pushed on, even when her spiritual muscles were sore she saw the end result of spiritual strength. She knew the benefit of building her muscles and knew that she would require them throughout her Christian walk.

Dignity is defined as the state or quality of being worthy of honour or respect. It is earned. When you put in the time and effort to change from who you were to who God wants you to be, you deserve to be respected and honoured as a child of God in a way that says, "Look what God has done in my life," "I'm not who I used to be. I am changing." God honours humility because in your humility God gets the glory for all things. When you know that you rely on God for everything, your position can't be anything but strong and secure. The woman of virtue is one with confidence and faith in God.

As parents, our children have needs, and our job is to provide the needs of our children, whether they are financial, emotional, or otherwise. Our children have faith that whatever they need from us as their parents we will supply. I highly doubt that your child lays awake in bed all night worrying about how you are going to pay your house payment next week. If God says, "If you then, being evil, know how to give good gifts to your children, how much more will your Father who is in heaven give good things to those who ask him?" (Matthew 7:11, NJKV). Then just as it is your job to provide for your children, we are the children of God, and His promises are to supply all our needs according to His riches in glory (Philippians 4:19).

All my children used to do this thing where they loved to jump off of the steps and into my arms. They would say, "Mommy, catch me!" and as soon as they said it, they jumped. How did they know that I would catch them? I'm sure it had a lot to do with their confidence in me and the fact that I proved to be trustworthy before. They knew I would never leave them to fall. That is the very same trust that we, as women of virtue, need to develop in God. "Lord, catch me!" and without a second thought know that He will be there for you. You can rejoice over the future when you know who holds your future in His hands. This isn't a promise of no more trials or tribulations, nor is this a promise that you won't be a target for Satan. This is, however, a guarantee of never having to endure the great pressures that come against you on your own. You have a trainer who is willing to strength train you so you are prepared and able to withstand the pressures of life.

Woman of virtue, rejoice over your future, be glad that you are not where you were, even if you are not where you want to be. Rejoice, knowing that you are prepared or preparing for the days to come and that you are not held down or bound by the hands of the enemy because you have found freedom in Christ Jesus. Of course, the woman of virtue would rejoice in her future because she is confident that better days are coming, and even if she can't see a brighter future here on Earth, she rejoices anyways, having confidence that there is better after this life.

"She opens her mouth in skillful and godly Wisdom, and on her tongue is the law of kindness [giving counsel and instruction]" (Proverbs 31:26 AMP).

A woman who opens her mouth with skillful and

godly wisdom is a woman who is careful about her words and one who is quick to seek guidance from God about her approach to things. As God begins to change you, you will come to notice how He surrounds you with people who will encourage you and people who require encouragement themselves.

Women love to gossip. Yes, I know not all of us gossip, but a lot of us do. Have you ever had a situation where you spoke to someone about an issue and maybe you just wanted to express your feelings of frustration and, instead of that person listening, it ends up being a session of gossip? They become critical and judgemental and now you feel it would have been better keeping it to yourself because you end up feeling worse than you did before you spoke. I will admit that there were times in my past when if someone came to me about an issue, especially if it was a sensitive heartfelt issue, my approach was to criticize. I never took the time to think about how to encourage someone in a way that was uplifting and supportive. I thought my opinions were valuable, otherwise they wouldn't be coming to me, right? I spoke many times based on emotions and how I would address the issue if it were me, apart from God's wisdom. Over the years, as God began to change my heart, mind, and spirit, I began to become sensitive to the fact that we are all sinners and, apart from God's grace and mercy, we all have the ability to fall.

As God began to open my eyes, I was able to encourage people and, with skillful and godly wisdom, give them a point of view from a loving God's perspective. This method can be used in every situation, no matter the issues or problems someone may come to you with. As a woman of virtue, your approach must be from a godly wisdom point of view. What this means is if you are approached by someone, whether it be a sister, brother, cousin, friend, or co-worker with a problem, don't be one to gossip and fuel the fire. Approach every situation with gentleness and love. Be trustworthy and willing to listen; and when God leads you, give advice that will help the individual. Don't advise based on your feelings, but be eager to give godly wisdom that is sought through the Word of God or through your prayers.

You may not realize it now, but your change in becoming a woman of virtue will impact the lives of many around you. God will begin to use you in ways you would never imagine. Your godly wisdom may be all someone needs to hear to change their mind from a suicide. Your godly wisdom may be all someone needs to hear to stop them from filing for divorce. Your godly wisdom may be all a teenage girl needs to hear before deciding to give her virginity to her boyfriend. Your godly wisdom may be all that someone who is ready to give up needs to hear to keep pushing on. Your godly wisdom may be all someone needs to finally make the decision to accept Christ as Lord and Saviour of their life. Woman of virtue, open your mouth with skillful and godly wisdom, and have the law of kindness on your tongue.

"A fool gives full vent to his anger, but a wise man keeps himself under control" (Proverbs 29:11). Your approach and how you interact and respond to others will make a difference in how people view and respect you. Oh boy, I was a vulgar one when I became angry. It took a whole lot to upset me and, for the most part, I was quiet-spirited, but when that right button was pushed, there was no telling what was going to come out of that volcano of mine. I had no self-control over the things I said or the way I behaved when I was extremely upset. I truly believe that part of being a woman of virtue is learning when and how to speak and when to be silent and humble. If people don't perceive you as a woman with godly wisdom, chances are they will not receive the words of wisdom you have to offer.

If you are a woman with children, godly wisdom is imperative. Your children are going to need to be reared in godly wisdom, and as they grow it is only the wisdom of God that will bring you through raising them in each stage of their life. When they finally become adults, if you think it's going to be resting time for you, think again. They are still going to require wisdom for stages in adulthood, so your job as a virtuous mother will not end when your children become adults. This is why it is necessary for you to be prepared with godly wisdom so that you can guide the ones who look up to you for support and direction.

They say that with age comes wisdom; however, it is not always so. There are many people who become older but lack wisdom and understanding. Wisdom comes through the lessons learned from your experiences and your ability to use your past experiences to learn and grow into a better person.

Wisdom is something that you can pass on to others so they can learn from you. It may be that they learn not to take the same wrong paths or that they learn how to survive through a rough time in their life. In all, the importance of having godly wisdom is good for you but it is also important to help others. "Blessed is the man who finds wisdom, the man who gains understanding" (Proverbs 3:13). "The mouth of the righteous man utters wisdom, and his tongue speaks what is just" (Psalms 37:30).

Never be afraid to speak with wisdom in kindness and in love. For a long time, I was what we call the "passive Christian." One who had wisdom and understanding of the right, but who would see loved ones going down the wrong pathway and be too afraid to speak up, fearing what they would think or that I would then become less likeable. Over the years, I've come to recognize that speaking what's just should override my desire to feel popular. There is a way to speak what's just without making others feel judged or condemned, so you have to be careful with your approach.

As a woman of virtue, your job is to love those around you so much that you desire to see better for them than what the enemy has planned for their lives. You know, sometimes it's the righteous (and I don't mean self-righteous, there is a difference) that see beyond what the natural eyes present, and that is why it is important to intervene when God leads you. Speak what's just but also pray for those around you. Wisdom is also to know when to speak in quietness by praying for your loved ones that they themselves would come to have wisdom and knowledge of God's perfect plan and will for their lives.

Proverbs 1:7 says that "The fear of the LORD is the beginning of knowledge, but fools despise wisdom and discipline." Wisdom and discipline actually work hand-in-hand. There is a dedication that it takes to walk in godly wisdom and also to seek godly wisdom. The Bible says in *all* your ways acknowledge Him and He will direct your path (Proverbs 3:6). Wisdom is not a one-time gift that is given once you have dedicated your life to walk in righteousness. This wisdom is a process of continual thinking, seeking, and acting according to God's lead.

As you pray for wisdom over the lives of others, don't forget about yourself. Pray daily that God will lead you in the way of godly wisdom. Let wisdom be the leading force of your every action and desire. I can guarantee that if I were to ask you to look back over your life at some of the decisions you have made or wrong paths you have taken, you would probably admit that had you waited for wisdom to play a role in those decisions you would have probably chosen differently.

In order for you to open your mouth with skillful and godly wisdom, you must recognize that it begins with the fear of the Lord. Woman of virtue, walk in wisdom and seek understanding so that your tongue will be filled with the law and your actions will display a woman who has chosen the way of the law. Live out your life as a woman with great insight.

CHAPTER 9

"She looks well to how things go in her household, and the bread of idleness (gossip, discontent, and self-pity) she will not eat."
(Proverbs 31:27, AMP)

I
t's amazing how God will bring certain people into your life when He is transforming you into what He wants you to become. Over the years, I have had the privilege to interact, give, and take advice from different wives and mothers older and younger than myself. And one thing has become very clear and evident to me, and that is being a woman who is dedicated to God takes effort, persistence, and determination.

At some point or another, as wives, we may feel overwhelmed with what seems to be an impossible mission assigned by God. Taking care of a household is no easy task. We are stretched thin, and it is difficult not to fall into the self-pity mode when we feel like all we do is give, give, give, and all our household does is take, take, take. I can't tell you the countless amounts of times I have heard women say, "I can't do this anymore!" I admit that I am one of those women.

The woman of virtue is a woman who desires structure and order within her home. I know for myself that one of my biggest pet peeves is walking into my home after a long day of work, only to be greeted by chaos—shoes scattered at the front door, toys on the floor, socks left in the family room, and an unkempt kitchen. I love to keep a clean house. Nothing makes me more relaxed and happy than a home that says, "I'm cared for."

When some of my children started getting older, it became harder to control the environment in my home. I thought it would have been easy, assuming that they would just grow up and mimic what they saw me doing. Boy, was I wrong about that. It took a long time to get them on the same page, and even when they were, it took constant reminders of what I thought they should have known by then. The makeup of everyone's family is different, and the structure of every home is personalized with a little twist of preference. But however your family is structured, one thing is important across the board when it comes to being a woman of virtue—it is your *job* to overlook how things go in your household.

Your household says a lot about who you are as a woman. This is your safe haven, your place of comfort and rest. Is your home well-kept? When someone walks through your front door, what is the first impression of your home that they get? If your house was a presentation, how would you rate it overall for cleanliness, organization, and structure? Most importantly, how evident is it that your home is a place that the Holy Spirit of God resides? Ask yourself, "Is my house in order?"

As I struggled to get my lazy teens to see the importance of keeping the house the way I did when they were little, I had to think of different ways to keep things organized. I had to make sure each able-bodied person was completing their assigned tasks. I went from plastering reminders in every room I knew was going to be occupied by them at some point or another in the day to setting alarm reminders on my phone, to ensuring I double-checked their chores were done, to taking away privileges if they had not done them, to being a constant tick on their backs, until they got the point. Believe it or not, there are still times when it's a struggle to get everyone to do their part. It's about being consistent and never ever giving up. Sure, I have felt like going on strike, but God gently reminded me that that's not the right way. The woman of virtue looks well to how things go in her household. This is not a one-time thing, this is a wife thing, a mother thing, and this is something that is a part of who we are. Think for a minute, if you have children, who do the children come to most often, if not all the time, when they are hurt or sick? Mommy. If there are school papers or homework to complete? Mommy. If there are pieces of clothing missing or a tough stain needs to be removed from their shirt? Mommy. What about when they're hungry or in need of something? Most likely, Mommy. If you have no children, then take a look at your husband, is it not relatively the same thing? "Hun, what is here to eat?" "Babe, did you wash my white shirts?" "Sweetheart, I'm not feeling so good, can you bring me something?" We women keep things together, in order, organized, and structured. So yes, woman of virtue, *you* are the one who has to look well into how things go in your household because *you*, my friend, set the pace.

The first time my husband and I went into financial hardship, it was a struggle, and at one point we went from treading water to what felt like drowning. Everything seemed too hard to control, and nothing seemed to be changing fast enough. No matter how hard I tried, things kept getting worse. One day, I decided it was just too hard, so I quit trying. Let's just say that my *choice* to quit ultimately left us in a state of needing resuscitation. Metaphorically speaking, we drowned. As a result of my giving up, things got from bad to worse to impossible. Years later, looking back at where God brought us from, I give all glory to God. I learned not to make the *choice* to eat the bread of idleness (self-pity). I could have *chosen* to not let my situation get the best of me, and instead of giving up and believing that it was never going to change, I could have looked into how it *could* change and then rely on God to show us a way out, which He eventually did. Once we came to realize the importance of putting things into God's hands, things turned around and change began to take place.

Woman of virtue, do not give your time to idleness. Laziness has no business hanging around the woman of God. There is too much for you to do, too much to prepare and get ready for. God is counting on you, your husband is counting on you, and your children are counting on you. You have no time to ingest the poison of gossip, discontent, and self-pity, they do nothing for your soul but bring destruction. Yes, I get that our lives can be overwhelmingly consumed with responsibilities within our household, but remember God has given you the capability to complete your tasks. To whom much is given, much will be required (Luke 12:48).

There is another side to a woman who looks well to how things go in her household. It is very easy to pick up on the things we feel are the duties of others that are not being fulfilled. As Christian wives and mothers, many women feel that their husbands lack leadership qualities, whether it is in the spiritual realm or physical realm. I have heard women say that they feel like their spouse lacks spiritual guidance from God, and due to that unsure feeling, they have difficulty submitting. Here is my question to you: Has God given you the responsibility to ensure that your husband is in complete submission to Him? What is it that God expects from you? You do your part, pray about the part you cannot control, and leave the rest to God.

There is a difference between looking into how things go in your household and being a woman of dictatorship and control. This is the part of your role that you can misunderstand. You are not ordained as the head of your home, drill sergeant, or ruler of all. While looking and ensuring there is structure and order in your home, you must have meekness and humility. Find a gentle way of approaching issues that are unsatisfactory in your household. For example, if the issues surround finances, and you feel like your husband and you are not on the same page, pray first about how you should approach him, find verses of Scripture to back up your thought, then make suggestions and discuss alternatives. Learn to compromise. After coming to a decision, make a date with your spouse in a non-stressful environment to review what you guys have discussed and evaluate if your plan was in fact effective and, if not, revise and try again.

It is a fact that it may take several trials and errors to finally come to a place where you feel your household is set up to your ideal vision of what you want it to be, then again that may never be your reality. Your ultimate responsibility is to look well into how things go in your household and make the changes you can and pray about the ones you can't. God sees the sincerity of your heart and, as long as you give it over to Him, you will start to see the results of your steadfast efforts.

Children can be the most challenging, especially when trying to rear them in a world of such corruption and rebellion against God. Oh, how I have laboured in prayer for my children. I have endured the great challenge of the transition from child to teen, and with each phase of my children's lives I would grow more anxious about the challenges and stresses they would face. Being a mother of six children, how could I impact their lives so that they will grow to fear and love the Lord with all their hearts and minds? I struggled with learning the right things to set in place to ensure they would make the right decisions. How would they deal with peer pressure? Would they stand up for the truth, even if it made them the odd one out? How do I raise them in a God-fearing way when the poisonous world opposes everything ordained by God? For a long time I had anxiety. I worried that my precious little children would be influenced and tarnished by the world's ideas of life. The more I saw the Word of God fulfilling itself, the more anxiety I would have. I struggled and wondered many times how I would go up against a world that had such great influences in music, money, fame, and entertainment. Public schools and governments that tell and teach our children that there is no God, that we live how we want, with no regulation or guidance, a world that believes anything goes.

How would I deliver the truth of a God whom they could not see? After many tears of desperation, I realized my approach was all wrong. It was *not* my job to go up against the world, that job was too great for me, and that's why there was so much anxiety. I then began to pray for my children in a very different way. I prayed that God would reveal Himself to my children. I lived a life that was truthful so my children were able to see the realness of God's ability to transform. My faults and wrongdoings were naked, there was no shame attached to my mistakes, only lessons of God's grace and ability to forgive and change. I prayed that God would help me to be a great example and that in every challenging situation my children would face that I would know how to approach them with a heart of love and forgiveness, just as God had shown me. I had to learn not to be judgemental and critical, but to approach my children with uncompromising truth when it came to situations that opposed the Word of God. Did they always want to hear it? No. Did they always believe it? No. But guess what? That was not my concern. My concern was to plant the seed, give it water, and fertilize it. The timing of the harvest was all up to God, so I did all that I could do.

Jesus gives a parable in Matthew 13 about seeds that were sown. The parable has many scenarios that could be used to illustrate His point, but let's just look at it as sowing seeds in our children. Jesus talks about a sower who sowed seeds and some fell by the roadside, and the birds came and ate them up (speaking to our children sometimes may seem like that, in one ear out the other), other seeds fell on rocky ground, where they had not much soil; and at once they sprang up, because they had no depth of soil. But when the sun rose, they were scorched and because they had no root, they dried up and withered away (when trying to get through to your child you may say, "I think they heard me, but did they truly get it? Will they listen and take heed to my direction?") Other seeds fell among thorns, and the thorns grew up and chocked them (your children are taught the way of Truth, but they live in a world full of evil, conspiracy, controversy, disobedience, and rebellion towards God), other seeds fell on good soil, and yielded grain, some a hundred times as much as was sown, some sixty times as much, and some thirty.

Are you sowing the truth of God on good soil? Prepare the soil by reading the word of God, pray with and for your children. Place them in other environments that will counteract the negative, such as the youth group at your church, church services, Christian schools, etcetera. Fast and pray for your children. Keep on feeding the truth of God's Word to them in every situation and opportunity you get. I encourage you to read all of Matthew 13. Woman of virtue, the point here is that it is God who will finish what you have started, but *you* have to prepare the soil so that it is good and ready to receive the seed (God's truth), then water it (with love, patience, forgiveness, living by example, prayer and fasting, setting the right environment), then watch it flourish and grow in God's perfect timing.

We cannot force our children to believe or accept God and His ways. We can only live by way of example and pray that God softens their hearts and opens their minds to receive Him as Lord of their lives. We are living in a troubled world with no direction, one that has convinced itself that order is not necessary and that the universe created itself, one that believes there is no need for a Saviour because we can save ourselves. Woman of virtue, we cannot afford to give up on directing our children out of darkness and into the light. Part of looking well to how things go in your household is to be aware of what your children are consuming through what they watch, listen to, who they hang out with, and what interests they have when outside of your home. Be a parent who is aware. Granted, you will never be able to know everything at every moment, but your efforts to be involved in the lives of your children are your responsibility.

"Her children rise up and call her blessed (happy, fortunate, and to be envied); and her husband boasts of and praises her [saying],"
(Proverbs 31:28)

We live in a world that finds much pleasure in entertainment, and some find themselves idolizing these entertainers, whether it is an actor from a favourite TV show or a talented singer. People tend to hold them to a high standard and gain respect and appreciation for them without ever really knowing who these people are. Then, when something comes up in the news that exposes these individuals' imperfections, people are shocked and disappointed as though they were unaware that these people are humans, too.

As little girls, we develop a habit of idolizing

complete strangers and engaging in the lives of these female entertainers who appear to be unflawed. Yet, the very women surrounding us in our daily lives, like the mothers, grandmothers, sisters, and aunties, those whom we've known and grown with, have very little influence on who we want to be when we grow up. We women of virtue have a responsibility to hold to a higher standard than what we see portrayed in the lives of celebrities. We should be an example of who our young girls want to be when they grow up. We should lead by example.

The woman of virtue's children rise up (grow up) and call their mother blessed. The children have come to recognize and appreciate the value of a godly woman. A woman, wife, mother, friend who has displayed steadfast love and patience, one who is encouraging and prayerful, one who is ready and willing to guide and give direction, one who says, "You're wrong, but I love you anyway," one who displays the unshakeable, unchangeable agape love of Christ Jesus. A woman of virtue, what an example to follow, a woman who has displayed the naked truth of her imperfections, yet is eager and determined to allow God to change her continually. What better way to show God's hand of forgiveness and love. What good is it to appear as someone who knows it all, someone who is condemning and fault-finding? The best way to show our children that we know where they're coming from is to openly admit that we ourselves have been there.

There is a saying that children are a product of their environment, and I have seen firsthand how true this statement is. For many years, my mother has fostered children, and these children are of many different nationalities and come into care for many different reasons, but one thing each child brings is an example of how they lived at their homes prior to coming into my mother's home. It didn't take very many days to analyze the type of life some of these children were subjected to. You could tell the ones who yearned for love and attention, the ones who were given too much responsibility for their age, the ones who were left to care and guide themselves, the ones whose innocence had been stolen away, and the ones who were subjected to things a child should not have to be subjected to. These children had need for love and direction.

It is obvious that a person can only give what they possess within. In Genesis 1:11-12 God says, "'Let the earth bring forth grass, the herb that yields seed, and the fruit tree that yields fruit according to its kind, whose seed is in itself, on the earth; and it was so. And the earth brought forth grass, the herb that yields seed according to its kind, and the tree that yields fruit, whose seed is in itself according to its kind. And God saw that it was good." (Genesis 1:1-12, NKJV). A pear tree will not bear apples because God has designed seeds to reproduce their own kind. My point here is that your children learn what they see. They become a product of the environment in which they grow. They say the apple doesn't fall far from the tree. Woman of virtue, your children are watching. What seeds are you planting within your environment? Are you planting rocks and expecting grapevines to flourish?

The desire to be like someone else is birthed out of admiring something about the individual. Whether it be a particular look, body type, personality, fame, or characteristic, the person who has desires to be like the other in some way has envied something that that person possesses. One of two things may happen: this individual will either strive for the same kind of achievement, or they will forever begrudge the individual for having something they want to possess. Envy can be a good thing with great outcomes when it comes to someone looking at the life of another and wanting to better himself, or it can be a bad thing if jealousy is attached and if one wishes for the demise of the person who possesses something they desire to have. In Proverbs 31:28 the Amplified Bibles says, "Her children call her blessed (happy, fortunate, and to be envied)." This envy is an envy of desire to be like a woman who has made it through the difficult times, one whose life has been transformed by the grace of God, a woman who was a flawed ruby but who went through the process of refinement like gold and has come out on the other side with her head held high, determined to keep on pushing through life's challenges. She's a God-fearing, hardworking, loving wife and mother, a woman of strength and dignity, a woman of prayer, and a woman who plants the seed of faith in everything she does, a woman of all traits, one who protects her family and loved ones with scarlet, someone who prays for and loves others, and one who has a heart of forgiveness. She is the merchant ship that leads by God's direction. She directs her distaff to the spindle and allows God to take control of her life. She gives to the needy her love, her support, her time, and her devotion, whatever is needed. She's a woman of strong character and high morals. She is a protector and a spiritual guard for her household. She is a woman of wisdom and kindness. Wow! What a woman! Why wouldn't your child/children rise up and feel like God's blessings are upon your life?

Woman of virtue, this is exactly what God wants from you. Your daughters should envy you and strive to bear the fruit of the seeds you have planted within them. Your sons should envy you and desire to find a God-fearing woman who displays your characteristics. The seeds planted in your son will still produce the product of what you sow; your gentleness, love, and kindness will produce a great man in him. Your prayers, over and for his life will produce who he is to become in Christ.

A proud husband will always boast about the greatness of his woman. There is something about a marriage when the husband and wife are living out their rightful role the way God intended them to. A husband of leadership and a wife who is submissive under the order of God equals an indestructible, powerful union in marriage. It may be a situation where your husband is not quite there yet, but I assure you, continue to stand in prayer believing God, and God will continue to work in him. A saying I hear often is "a happy wife makes a happy life." There also is a saying that "behind every good man is a good wife." Every marriage requires a balance. Marriage is about giving, selflessness, and the ability to put the other in front of yourself. When a marriage is broken, if you examine it carefully it all boils down to one or both individuals being selfish, which ultimately causes a wall to be built up and a brokenness in the communication.

Woman of virtue, God is the foundation. When a house is built, the builder starts with a foundation so that as the materials that frame the home are being formed, the house does not crumble. Wherever your husband is in his Christian walk, that's okay, we don't all learn to crawl at the same age. Pray and let God take over. When a house is being built, there is a blueprint or floor plan, which outlines in detail what the end product is supposed to look like. However, it is not the person who draws the floor plan that builds the house. An architect draws it and then he passes it over to someone capable of doing the task. Your responsibility is to give the floor plan to the professional, and the professional will complete the work. You may have an idea of how you want your marriage to be or how you envision your husband to be as the man of the house, and there is nothing wrong with having a blueprint for the kind of marriage you desire. Hand it over to the Master of creation to set a strong foundation and begin building.

Your husband will boast within himself and to others when he sees your love for God and your commitment to him and your family. Even if your husband is not at the place where God wants him to be, your commitment in standing strong for your marriage and your family will bring change within your home. "He who finds a

[true] wife finds a good thing and obtains favour from the Lord" (Proverbs 18:22). I have seen men who boast about their wives. It is such a refreshing thing to see the way their eyes light up and the smile on their faces as they express their appreciation for the woman by their side. I know at times it may seem like your efforts go unnoticed, but believe me, your husband sees and knows the great value he has in his wife. Should you walk out and for a month and leave him to do all that you do, you will soon see just how much he can't do without you. God knew it was not good for men to be alone, so He made women. Regardless of whether it is expressed to you or not, remember that as you do all that you do, you are doing it as unto the Lord, so your reward comes from Him.

Some men have a hard time expressing feelings of gratitude, and some may choose to show gratitude in a different way. I encourage you to be sensitive to the different ways your husband may be boasting or praising you for being who you are. It may be the silent kiss on your forehead, the soft stroke of your hair, the rubbing of your feet, or just the extra little things he doesn't usually do around the house but decides to do, periodically. It may even be letting you sleep in while he decides to get the kids ready one day. All communication does not have to be verbal. Appreciate even the small things that may seem like nothing at the time. Your husband will take great pride knowing he has a wife that is committed to living a life for the mission and purpose of the Lord.

CHAPTER 10

❧

"Many daughters have done well, but you excel them all." (Proverbs 31:29, NKJV)

There is no competition against the woman of virtue. If you have chosen the right way, who can compete with you? It is a known fact that even in the Biblical days men struggled with wandering eyes and curiosity that led them into the danger zone of lust and sinful desires. Let's not be foolish and ignore Satan's task to try and lure and tempt our men to give into the feelings of lust and sexual immorality. King Solomon, being as wise as he was, warned men several times about the effects of giving into these temptations. Solomon warns about the loose woman in Proverbs 5. The goal was to prevent men from falling into the trap of a seductive woman. Satan is the master of deception. It is when issues arrive in a marriage that the serpent comes in with something that may appear to be more appealing. He sets the stage with the right circumstances at the right time. In no way am I implying that if a marriage is in trouble that a husband will go out and commit adultery, but what I am saying is be conscious and aware because Satan has a way of sneaking in unexpectedly, and if given the right opportunity he will take advantage of it. Let's face it, there are women out there waiting to be the forbidden fruit for a man who is hungry for more.

Work towards being the best well-rounded woman you can be. After all, you are not alone; the spirit of God resides with you and is able to guide and help you, all that you are required to do is work in accordance and obedience to His Word. It is a fact that many will read this book but only few will actually grasp the true meanings, use the knowledge given, and act upon the wisdom given throughout this book. Proverbs 31:29 says, "Many daughters have done well but you excel them all." There are many women who make good Christians, good wives, good mothers, friends, sisters, aunties, cousins, and are just genuinely good people, but the woman of virtue excels them all because her desires are to live out a life in accordance to God's Word and His order.

I watched a message from Joyce Meyers entitled "Check Your Motives," and she said something that stuck with me—"Do what's right because it's right, even if you never get the results." Being a woman of virtue is not to gain recognition or to obtain favour in the sight of God and others. Being a woman of high moral values and standards should be something you desire because you understand your worth and the value that God has placed on you. Your understanding should give you the desire to express your value and worth in the things you say and do. Is it easy to obtain? No. Is it impossible to sustain? No. You are the one who has to make the conscious decision to pursue a life that reflects your highest potential and be that woman who is far more precious than jewels and whose value is far above rubies or pearls. It is obtainable, but you have to set out to get it, no matter what your circumstances and situations are.

You have the choice to submit totally and completely to God's way of doing things or you may choose the way of man, which has proven to fail, time after time after time. The Amplified Bible says, "Many daughters have done virtuously, nobly, and well [with the strength of character that is steadfast in goodness], but you excel them all." Let's look at the definition of *steadfast*. Steadfast means resolutely or dutifully firm and unwavering, loyal, faithful, committed, devoted, dedicated, dependable, reliable, steady, true, constant, staunch, solid, trusty. In order to live out a life as a virtuous woman, you are required to be committed to continuously walking in right standing with God. You must be a woman with high awareness of your moral standards and values, and there is no place for compromise. Be steadfast, consistent, determined, faithful, and longsuffering. This is no walk in the park.

Committing to living your life as a woman of virtue is no easy task, but it is one that is rewarding. Just think about the satisfying feeling you will have when you come to realize and understand how empowering it is to have control over your responses to your circumstances instead of your circumstances having control over you. Let me explain that statement a little more. As a woman of virtue, you are in right standing with God; you've made the choice to live a life of righteousness, no matter what your circumstances are. Morality can be compromised because people struggle with a weakness, or someone may be angered by a circumstance or situation which then causes rebellion against God.

So, here you are as a woman of virtue, you have decided to follow the way of the Lord, regardless of your outward situations. You choose righteousness instead of rebellion; you choose forgiveness instead of malice; you choose love instead of hate; you choose trust instead of doubt; you choose prayer instead of worry; and you choose God's ways instead of man's ways. Just think, is that not freeing? I am sure you know at least one person who has lived a life controlled by their current or past circumstances, and they appear to be in bondage. The bondage may be expressed through substance abuse, promiscuity, anger, bitterness, depression, hatred, envy, rage, or rebellion. These people are the ones who are controlled by their life circumstances and situations. When a conscious decision is made to live out a life of moral standards and the choices are made based on God's Word and not life's circumstances, marriages can be saved, children can be saved, and financial situations can be turned around. People can experience healing, and many changes can and *will* happen. We are not supposed to be in submission to our circumstances, our circumstances are supposed to be in submission to us. The woman of virtue has excelled others because of her faith. She has chosen to submit her all to God, and because of her faithfulness God's blessings are upon her and her household.

The desire to live as a woman of virtue has to come from deep in the core of your being. There is a deeper desire in you to be all that God created you to be. King Lemuel's mother asked, "Who is he who can find her?" obviously implying that such a woman is hard to come by. As a woman who made a choice to proclaim Christianity as her faith, why would you not desire to serve the Lord wholeheartedly? This is our purpose, right? I am trying to get you to take a deeper look and ask yourself what sinful nature are you unwilling to let go of? What is holding you back from fulfilling a life lived out as a woman of virtue?

The challenge is to excel beyond the norm. Let's have peace and dominion in our homes, let's have love and laughter in our homes, let's have lasting marriages in our homes, let's be praying for all things in every circumstance and situation with all submission to God. Don't be quick to judge,quick to anger or take revenge, but be conscious of the sacrifice that Christ Himself gave. He did it expecting nothing in return. There is no repayment plan for the ultimate sacrifice of Christ.

Woman of virtue, know your worth, be excited about your efforts, and recognize your progress. You may not be where you want to be, but celebrate where God has brought you from and acknowledge that He can lead you to where you need to be. Strive to be your best; don't settle for the average. Become the one that has excelled them all!

> *"Charm and grace are deceptive, and beauty is vain, but a woman who reverently and worshipfully fears the Lord, she shall be praised!"*
> *(Proverbs 31:30)*

There is a saying that beauty is only skin deep, meaning that one's character is more important than her appearance. We, as women, take a lot of time putting together an image of ourselves. We take time to comb our hair, put on matching clothes with the matching shoes, we have the purse, and we even find the jewelry to match our apparel. What would happen if we were just as concerned about the presentation of our attitudes and the characteristics we display on a daily basis? What if our words were considered as important as picking out clean clothing? Or what if our display of love and patience was as important as adding the jewelry and matching shoes? Why are we not as concerned about the person we are on the inside as we are about the way we present ourselves on the outside? Remember the fig tree?

The fig tree's appearance looked just right but,

upon taking a closer look, the truth was revealed that it was a fake. Woman of virtue, nothing is more beautiful than a woman with a heart that loves the Lord and is committed to living a life for His purpose and service. The beauty you display should be that of a woman who is well-rounded. Having charm alone is not going to cut it. While this may fool a few for a while, the deep-rooted attitudes will come out given the right situation and circumstance.

I had a meeting one day with a few ladies. We were reading a book called *Wives After God's Own Heart* by Elizabeth George, and the topic of discussion was our attitude and being mindful of the ways in which we speak to our husbands. A Scripture reference that I used was Proverbs 25:11 which said, "A word fitly spoken and in due season is like apples of gold in a setting of silver." The illustration I used was a silver bowl and some fake apples that I sprayed gold. I used a nice shiny silver dish and nice shiny golden apples. Can you picture how beautiful it looked? As those shiny apples of gold sat nicely in the silver dish on the table, we continued our discussion, and we spoke about the difficulty we had at times controlling our tempers and watching what we say when we become irritated with our spouses. As we continued to talk I finished the demonstration by throwing two black rotten apples in with the beautiful gold apples. Guess what stuck out the most? Although the golden apples outnumbered the black ones, it was the black ones that stuck out the most. Beauty is vain, *if* it is only to deceive people to perceive you to be someone you are not. On the outside a person may appear like golden apples in a silver setting, but on the inside his or her attitudes and behaviours are like the rotten apples. Beauty on the outside will never be able to outlive the beauty on the inside.

We live in a world today where women seem to want to fix their outer appearance, whether it be breast implants, butt implants, tummy tucks, facelifts, or anti-aging products. The trend is to look your best on the outside. This is exactly what Proverbs 31:30 is referring to in saying charm and grace is deceptive and beauty is vain [because it is not lasting]. Think about this. All this time and money spent to create a projected illusion, yet many, though looking good on the outside, are dying on the inside. Wake up! The outer body is only for a time, it is your spirit that lives on. This is where you need to invest and spend your time.

Develop your personality, work within yourself to become better from the inside out, and the outer beauty will follow. There is a sincere beauty that flows out of a woman with a genuine heart, who fears and loves the Lord. There is something about that soft answer that turns away wrath, that giving heart that's willing to pray for others, and the understanding that we all fall short of the glory of God. There is something about that truth that we can be angry but not sin, that spirit of kindness that refuses to gossip. There is just something about that woman, the woman of virtue who reverently and worshipfully fears the Lord.

I can remember as a little girl wanting to be like so

many "beautiful women" on TV. I remember admiring their hair, bodies, and thinking they had it all. As the years went by, some of these same women that appeared to have it all started to fall apart right before the eyes of the world. Some of them were in physically abusive relationships, some of them were involved in drugs, and some of them were wasting their lives on too much partying and foolishly spending money to the point where they lost everything. I can remember many times thinking to myself, "But she had everything." Here's the thing, no, she did not have everything. It was deceptive. She appeared as one thing but the reality is her outer appearance did not depict who she was on the inside. Many women spend time working on their outer appearance, but silently they are dying on the inside. That's the real reason for the drugs and alcohol, that's the real reason behind staying in a relationship where someone is using them as a punching bag, that's the real reason for continuing to spend millions of dollars trying to fix what they feel is wrong on the outside, and that's the reason it is never enough. The reason why they can't find the "fix it" is because they are wasting their time on the beauty that's vain.

If only people could see that all life experiences are meant to bring us through a period of growth. We are by nature prone to making mistakes because we are not made perfect. However, in our imperfections we are supposed to find tools that will prepare and develop us for our next steps in life. Developing inner beauty is about growing in our character and changing for the better. Maturing and becoming wiser will build stronger character traits that can then be used for better decision making and choices regarding our future.

What exactly does it mean to reverently and worshipfully fear the Lord? To have reverence is to have a feeling or attitude of deep respect tinged with awe. To be worshipful is to show worship (honour paid to God). There is something about a woman who has come to grips with her spiritual design to worship God. There is something about a humble spirit that recognizes that without a creator there can be no creation. It is so easy to live our lives on a daily basis as though we knew we were promised tomorrow. I have seen how quickly the perspective of an individual changes when they learn that their life has been shortened due to sickness and disease.

We spend a significant amount of our lives searching for ways to better our outer appearance and achieve those materialistic things that we believe will bring us a sense of achievement and accomplishment, but how many take time out to dwell on what counts the most? Our spirit is the only entity that outlives our physical body, and no matter how hard we work to achieve all the materialistic goals on this earth, they too have a date of expiry. It was in the lowest time of my life that I truly discovered the love of God and just how faithful He is. There was a time in my life when I experienced deep depression, yet everyone who saw me would tell me how beautiful my smile was and say that they always see me smiling, never knowing how much I was dying on the inside.

Why is it that we see so many women who appear to have it all together, yet through greater insight we find that so many are struggling with things that go deeper than the skin. Some struggle with depression, some with alcohol and drug abuse and some live a life of immorality. Why is it that beauty on the outside is just not enough? There is more to what we see in someone's outer appearance, that's why.

Genesis teaches that God made us all in His image, and if God is spirit before flesh, then guess what? So are we. Our spirit is the core of who we are and, sad to say, a lot of people do not acknowledge this. What a revelation it would be if we all recognize the imperativeness of developing spiritually because this is truly the only thing that really counts. You can spend all the time in the world eating right, taking care of your body by going to the gym, counting calories, wake up every day and put on your best business suit, do your makeup and the whole nine yards, but what value is it to you if your spirit is not right with the Lord?

My children asked me the question one day, how do I know that God is really real, and how do I know that what I believe is the truth about Heaven and Hell? While I could have said I know God is real because I feel him, or I could have pointed out the creativity of even the smallest insects and urged them into thinking there must be a God whose infinite wisdom created all things in Heaven and Earth, I didn't. My answer was this, "Let's say I am completely wrong. Let's say there is no God and everything I ever believed was not correct, and I die. What's the worst thing that could happen to me? But what if I don't believe in God and I was wrong? It will be too late when I die to change my mind."

Woman of virtue, "the fear of the Lord is the beginning of wisdom" (Psalm 111:10). "Be not wise in your own eyes; fear the Lord and depart from evil" (Proverbs 3:7). The woman of virtue is one who fears the Lord, and for that reason alone she is committed to living a life that is pleasing to God.

I am not suggesting walking around with your holier-than-thou hat on. While you're committed to living a life that is pleasing to God, there is a balance in that. What I am talking about is to have a heightened awareness that you are a spiritual being *first* before anything else, and for that reason spend time feeding that being and building strength in your spirit. Life happens and storms *will* come your way, whether physical, emotional, or financial, they will come. But if your spirit is weak, those life circumstances will be your demise. It can take one situation to bring someone from one extreme to the next, and usually all hope is lost to the one who has not spent time building a spirit that will stand firm in the midst of a storm. Your spirit is your foundation.

In Matthew 7, Matthew speaks regarding self-reflection and looking to fulfill the desires of one's heart. He then uses the metaphor of the wide and narrow gates and implores the people to take the narrow gate because the wide gate (the way of men) is the way to destruction, and many people choose this way. He then says that the narrow way (God's way) leads to life, and there are few that find it. He goes on to talk about being aware of false prophets and makes comparisons between the good and bad fruit. What he was doing here was warning that many will lead you astray if your eyes are not open. He then says that not everyone who calls upon the Lord in the day of judgement will be known to the Lord simply because they state what they have done here on Earth. If you do not have a personal relationship with the Lord, your good deeds on Earth mean *nothing*. Matthew speaks to the people and says that all who hear and put the things he has spoken about into action are "like a wise man who builds his house on the rock. The rain came down, the streams rose, and the winds blew and beat against the house; yet it did not fall, because it had its foundation on the rock. But everyone who hears these words of mine and does not put them into practice is like a foolish man who built his house on sand. The rain came down, the streams rose, and the winds blew and beat against that house, and it fell with *a great crash*" (Matthew 7:24-27).

If your foundation is not strong and the structure is built out of materials that are easily destroyed, your whole house will crumble because of the inability to withstand the pressures of a storm. Your body is the storage house of your spirit. Imagine a real house for a moment. There is the brick and underneath that is the framework along with the drywall and insulation. Everything a builder uses to build a house is used first and foremost to protect what is on the inside of the house. Can you see a house with no roof, no installation, and no walls?

While the outer structure is important, let's take a look on the inside. Imagine a house built on the outside, the framework and outer layout of the house looks just fine, but on the inside the toilets flood, no one cleans them, the dishes are never washed and put away, the house has never been dusted, the walls are cracking from the inside, all the windows have mold and mildew, and overall the upkeeping of the inside of the house has been neglected. If you have ever seen wood that has been wet, when the moisture absorbs into it after it sits for a while, it becomes warped and dry rot. When this happens, the wood is no longer strong, and it can't hold up under any pressure, so it breaks. If all these things were to happen to a house on the inside, it is only a matter of time before the outside would start to reflect the consequences of neglect on the inside. With a house that needs renovating, anything that requires fixing on the outside can be done as long as the structure still remains strong and sturdy inside.

Woman of virtue, build your house (your physical body), with a structure (your spirit) strong enough to withstand any storm. Live a life that is pleasing to God. Every day you wake up, be grateful for all the things that God has brought you through. Look at where He has taken you from, be grateful for everything, and worship Him in the good and in the bad because, whether good or bad, *he is still God.*

"A woman who reverently and worshipfully fears the Lord, she shall be praised!" (Proverbs 31:30).

The praise spoken about here is one of applause, compliment, and admiration. You *are* being watched and observed. The woman of virtue is a woman who can go through some storms and trials in her life and, in the midst of it all, still worship the Lord. Now *that* is a woman to admire. It says something about a woman with such character, one who is not shaken by her situation, a woman who does not waver, but who stands firm spiritually. I am talking about that woman of God who, when trials hit, displays the spirit of stability that is unshaken, and knows who her defender is. I am talking about that woman, the one who is unlike the others, the one who is like Jesus on the boat lying asleep peacefully while the storm is wreaking havoc, knowing God has it all under control. A woman of virtue who stands on God's track record, who knows His reputation, has seen Him work miracles before, does not doubt Him regardless of what things looks like. This type of woman is the one who shall be praised (applauded, commended, admired).

CHAPTER 11

"Give her of the fruit of her hands, and let her own works praise her in the gates."
(Proverbs 31:31)

You reap what you sow. Afterplanting a seed, there comes a time to reap of that harvest. I can remember while growing up that my mother used to take us grocery shopping. She would show us how to tell if a fruit was going to be a good one to buy. She would look for the ones with just the right colour and texture, even when it came to the watermelon she did some tapping thing and just knew which one was going to be the sweetest out of the bunch. I never quite understood that one, and still until this day I don't, but she was right every time.

Now that I am older and do the shopping for my own family, those things I have learned from my mother regarding picking the right fruit can't always be applied. It seems like the only choice nowadays in the grocery store is to pick the young and green and hope for the best. The fruits today are just not what they used to be. A lot of the time the fruit is picked well before it had time to mature, so we have these green, young fruits that are not ready to be eaten. Much like the young girls we see in our society today, everyone wants to grow up way too fast and be picked from the tree way before their time, with no real time to grow and mature.

If you have ever tasted the difference between a fruit that was given time to mature and one that has been prematurely ripped off the tree, there is a difference. I believe that just as the fruit requires the right amount of time to mature, we, as women, require that same process to mature into the right harvest, and in the right season we will flourish into all that God has created us to be. I think we can probably all attest to wanting to mature and grow up before our time. It is not until we get there that we wish we were younglings again. The one thing that I have learned as I matured into a woman is that who I am today is a combination of seeds planted along the arc of my life. I am a product of my decisions, and the things I have planted in the backyard of my life are the fruits that are growing in my orchard.

I can remember the days I lived my life in rebellion, doing things my way with no guidance or regard for how my actions would affect my life and those around me. I did whatever was pleasing to me at that particular time in my life. When a seed is planted, it needs to be in the right season and the soil must be ready to receive the seed, it can't be too moist or too dry. If the timing is not right then whatever is planted will not be received by the soil. Using my own life as an example, I can say that my soil was not prepared for the seed of virtue. I was once at a point in my life when I had been picked green. I had been through a lot that made me bitter and angry at the world for what I believed the world had done to me. My circumstances had come in and flooded my crops.

I grew up in the church, my parents were Christians, and I had been baptized at a young age. I was probably twelve years old or so and felt I was ready. As I began to grow and life started to unfold, I found myself straying away from my upbringings in the church. The reality was that I was never prepared for what was to come. A farmer knows that when a seed is planted he needs to be prepared for things that may come and pose danger to his crops. This includes things like weather extremes, the locust, and the worms. Although a farmer cannot stop these things, he will do his best to prepare for them.

The process of becoming a woman of virtue is about having soil that is prepared to receive the seeds and then giving it time to mature while understanding that extreme weather will come, and the locust and worms are also waiting to devour every seed that was planted. The challenge is to keep pushing on, even when it seems like nothing is changing, even when you feel like you have done enough and can't continue on. Seeds that are planted take some time to reach the surface. Just because you can't see the evidence of what is underneath the soil does not mean nothing is there.

While God began to do His work in me, I faced many challenges and the transition for me was very difficult. You can be the most perfect human on the face of the earth, and the moment you do wrong, it seems like that is the only thing everyone remembers about you. I say that to say this, the seeds planted from a past that you are not proud of are not the seeds that determine your future harvest. Those seeds can be uprooted and replaced, but you have to be willing to invest the time to replant a field full of seeds that will produce a great harvest.

Before a farmer begins to sow a seed, the farmer first cultivates the land. For change to come, woman of virtue, you must first prepare for it. This may entail taking time to really do some self-evaluation and some soul-searching. Look into who you are today, right now, and who you want to be. Are you satisfied with yourself or do you really understand that greater things lie within you? Once you have done a self-evaluation, make a decision. If you feel you are satisfied with yourself, I am sure there is still room for growth, and if you are not satisfied with yourself, then it's time for a change.

When a seed begins to grow it is called germination. This is the process of growing a new plant from a seed, and in this process the first thing to grow is the main root. How ironic, woman of virtue,that the root that requires growing before any other changes can be made in your circumstances and situation is *you*. You are that main root. It doesn't matter the person you were before, or what your past looked like, you can make a decision to uproot and replant with great expectations that once the new plant begins to flourish your harvest will be fruitful.

When a seed grows, the soil usually needs to be damp, warm, and dark. A dry seed will stay dormant until it soaks in some water, then it will start to grow. It is usually through the darkest days in someone's life that there is a desire for change. I can remember when I rebelled against God's will for my life, I kind of felt like Jacob wrestling with the angel, and it wasn't until my hip broke that I caved in and recognized my desire was for real change in my life. And, as Jacob did, I submitted to God and held onto Him saying, "I will not let go until you bless me!"

I have spoken to so many woman who are frustrated with their life situations, whether it be in their marriage, financial situation, issues with their children, or just wanting to find themselves and discover the next chapter in their lives, and one thing I have observed is in some way or another women, wives, mothers, we are all looking for something to change.

At one point or another, we have painted a picture of what our life should look like and what we want to achieve at a certain point in our lives, and when the evaluation of our lives does not add up with our expectations, we tend to feel aggravated with our life and its outcomes. We spend way too much time trying to plan out what our life will look like and the things we hope to possess but, woman of virtue, there is no value in the things we possess. The true value lies in the seeds planted in us that will then grow and become useful in helping us to deal with our challenges and situations in life as they come.

Let's look at someone who may have worked their whole life to achieve goals and accomplishments. They have the picture perfect life, including the car, the house, financial stability, the perfect relationship, and from the outside everything looks great. Then, out of what seems like nowhere, this same person has a nervous breakdown, or goes into deep depression, or commits suicide, or gets into drugs and alcohol. One of two things has happened. The right seeds were not planted on the right soil or the seed was dry and remained dormant. No value was placed on the seeds that lay within the individual and too much time was invested in possessions that satisfied the flesh for the moment.

I just love the way that God has already made up His mind about us, even before we began our journey in life. It was at a young age when God chose Jeremiah for an assignment. He informed Jeremiah that He had already formulated a plan for his life (Jeremiah 1:5). There are cases in the Bible where God would address someone using a different name than what they were previously called. He would use the name describing their potential and not who they were at that moment in time. You may have noticed throughout this book that I have addressed you as "woman of virtue," this was intentional so you

157

would understand that this is not about who you are now, it is about who you have the potential to become.

In Proverbs 31:10, the woman of virtue is described as capable, and I believe with everything in me that God has placed the capability in each and every one of us to live out a life as a virtuous woman. We have to be the ones to step into that destiny and see our life changes through our efforts for personal growth and development. We strive for everything else, why not strive to fulfill a life with a better you? Why not make the small changes daily that will build that solid foundation? Why not prepare for the storms of life instead of being caught off guard and fearing the flood?

We spend too much time trying to achieve the things that we will die and leave behind. Think for a minute how much you could impact the lives of the people around you if you lived your life based on Proverbs 31. What an example for many to see the power of a God-fearing woman, one who had a past and learned from her mistakes, one who has now come to recognize that without a solid foundation her house will collapse, and one who has her priorities straight. God first and all else will fall into place.

Can you see the impact that you will have? What an example for your daughters to see, what an example to teach your sons, what a wife to be proud of and admire and respect, most importantly, what a light in a dark world for all to see the capability in you through the trust you place in God. With His help and direction, those seeds that were planted will grow and soon you will reap the benefits of what was sowed. It is only through your efforts that this will become a reality for you. You cannot plant a thorn bush and expect a flourishing apple tree. What you sow is what you will harvest. "Give her the fruits of her hands, and let her own works praise her in the gates!" (Proverbs 31:31)

To transition from a woman of a sinful mindset to a woman of a high moral standard is a wonderful accomplishment. It is not a goal to set and once it is achieved that will be the end of it. It is a lifestyle change. What you used to do, you no longer desire. How you used to behave, you no longer feel right about. In everything you do, you now desire to communicate with God before you proceed. The woman of virtue understands that truly she is nothing without God, and she grasps that the very air she breathes is not of her own doing and would not be possible without Him. The works that is being referred to here is the individual efforts of this woman, and the praise is not a praise of arrogance or conceit. This praise is one of respect, admiration, and value for a God-fearing woman who has acknowledged that her sole purpose is to live a life of high moral standards and a life that others can see and want to duplicate. She is living a life that reflects a woman who was brought from a place of famine to feast, one who has experienced the struggles and the pains, the toil and turmoil, yet she is still standing as a woman who can praise God in the good times and the bad. She is that woman who when all hell breaks loose will awaken while her household sleeps and pray a prayer that will cause the very demons of hell to tremble. She is that woman who, even when sick, is capable of functioning as she looks to God for strength. She is a woman who sees no other option but to live by faith, *no matter what it looks like*!

A virtuous woman is truly hard to find, although many will read this book and desire to change, the truth is many will remain the same. I wrote this book to give a different perspective of the virtuous woman, a perspective that God laid on my heart. Before writing this book I had read Proverbs 31 on a number of occasions, but it was never revealed to me the way God revealed it to me as He inspired me to write. God has a greater purpose for us as women. We hold a power that we have not even began to tap into; the power I am talking about is life-changing. It is a game-changer for us, our marriages, our children, our finances, and our faith.

If you could only grasp the value that God has placed on each and every one of us and know that He doesn't desire to hold your past over your head. He doesn't want you living in condemnation. God does not want to see you struggle or live a life of emptiness and hopelessness. Ultimately, this is about an intimate relationship between you and the One who created you. The woman of virtue is one of great value because she understands her purpose. One will only feel devalued if they cannot see their worth. People who live a life of immorality are those who can only see the here and the now. We have to understand that we are spiritual beings even before we are physical beings, and as the Word says, "from dust we came and to dust we shall return."

My prayer is that many women will read this book and have a strong desire to live a life of high moral standards. Yes, I understand that we will all have desires to fulfill the flesh, and we will have the desire to achieve goals and accomplish things on Earth. This book is not about walking around like the holier-than-thou woman. This is to awaken something in your spirit so that you live a well-rounded life that has a foundation built on a solid relationship with the Lord.

Let the fruit of your hands be full with the fruit of the spirit—love, joy, peace, longsuffering, kindness, goodness, faithfulness, gentleness, and self-control. Let your own works praise (admire, compliment, applaud) you in your gates. Be the peacekeeper in your home, be the prayer warrior in your home, be the one that your children are confident in, so no matter what struggles or trials they face, they know coming to you means you are there to encourage and pray for and with them with no room for judgement. Be that wife that your husband is not afraid to fail around because he is certain you are there to help him get back up again. Be that neighbour that everyone knows will be the one to have encouraging words and a heart that loves. Be that sister, daughter, cousin, friend, the one who is prayerful at all times in every situation.

Plant the seeds within your home and be mindful of the locust that comes to destroy your crops. Look well to how things go within your household and do not allow the enemy to come in and take your marriage. Do not allow him to take your kids, and do not allow him to take your finances, your sanity, or your health. Grab hold of what God has given to you, see your worth and value as the precious gem that you are. Keep your faith, be strong, and be determined to live a life of purpose and fulfillment.

What are the seeds that are planted in your yard? What are the fruits that are in your hands? What things do you possess that are not perishable? Do you really know your self-worth? What are your works within your gates? Are you like the barren fig tree or are you producing good fruit?

"Give her of the fruit of her hands, and let her *own* works praise her in the gates." You, woman of virtue, what you sow is what you reap. "A capable, intelligent, and virtuous woman—who is he who can find her? She is far more precious than jewels and her value is far above rubies or pearls." (Proverbs 31:10) Jesus is sitting at the well waiting to meet you where you are. Will you drink from the living water? Will you drink from that fountain of water springing up into everlasting life? Or will your seeds be the seeds that sit in the dry soil and lie dormant in the ground? "Charm and grace are deceptive, and beauty is vain **but** a woman who reverently and worshipfully fears the Lord, **she** shall be praised (admired, complimented, applaud)" (Proverbs 31:30).

PRAYER

Heavenly Father, I thank you for the opportunity to be used by you to write a book of purpose and reflection. I pray that every woman who reads this book will come to know her worth and value in you. I pray for every woman who has ever felt devalued, unloved, and unworthy, that You will fill each one with your perfect love and acceptance. I pray that each one of these women will understand the power of your ability to meet them where they are in their lives. Help them to have a heightened acknowledgement of you in their individual circumstances and situations. I pray for change in their mindsets and desires.

Let us see a virtuous woman inside of each and every one of us. Show us our capabilities and give us the strength we need to endure life's challenges. Cover our homes, bless our marriages, bless our children, bless our finances, and bless our health. Keep the devourer out of our field of planted seeds, and give us every provision required to nourish each seed planted so we may reap a good harvest. Help us to recognize our need for you in all we do every single day. I pray that more and more women will desire and make the choice to live their lives as a virtuous woman, and as these desires come, Lord, you will make it a reality as we live a life more pleasing to you.

AMEN.

RESOURCES

www.biblegateway.org

www.dictionary.com

www.wikipedia.org

Connect with Stacy on Facebook and Twitter to share how this book has inspired you to walk as a woman of virtue.

Facebook Page: Life of a Proverbs 31 Woman: *Virtuous Woman*

Twitter: *@stacy_virtuous*

To book Stacy as a speaker at your next event, **send an email** to *lifeintheword1@outlook.com*.

www.ingramcontent.com/pod-product-compliance
Lightning Source LLC
Chambersburg PA
CBHW062106080426
42734CB00012B/2774